Related Macmillan titles

HOSPITALITY MANAGEMENT: CASE STUDY ASSIGNMENTS
Sally Messenger and Humphrey Shaw
WORKING IN THE HOTEL AND CATERING INDUSTRY
Sally Messenger

Financial Management

for the Hospitality, Tourism and Leisure Industries

Sally Messenger
Department of Management Studies for Tourism and Hotel Industries
University of Surrey

and

Humphrey Shaw
The Business School
University of North London

MACMILLAN

First published 1993 by
THE MACMILLAN PRESS LTD
Houndmills, Basingstoke, Hampshire RG21 2XS
and London
Companies and representatives
throughout the world

ISBN 0–333–58528–3

A catalogue record for this book is available
from the British Library.

Copy-edited and typeset by Povey–Edmondson
Okehampton and Rochdale, England

Printed in Great Britain by
Mackays of Chatham plc
Chatham, Kent, England

02 01 00 99 98 97 96 95 94 93
10 9 8 7 6 5 4 3 2 1

15.12.94

To our families and friends

Contents

Introduction

The main aim of this book has been to present the basic concepts and principles of financial management in a way that is easy to understand for students with no previous knowledge of the subject matter. It 's also hoped that the content will prove helpful to anyone intending to start a business in the hospitality, tourism, or leisure industries.

The text has been divided into three sections. Part I concentrates on explaining the different **financial statements** that are necessary in any business, and provides a basic foundation for the newcomer to financial management. An important part of a manager's role is **planning**, operating and controlling an enterprise, and so in Part II the focus is on analysing costs, decision making and budgetary control. Part III of the book involves the individual in **financial analysis**. This includes the interpretation of accounts, appraisal of capital investment programmes and the management of the working capital cycle.

The book has been based on a practical case study of two women who open the Croeso Hotel and leisure complex in North Wales. At the end of each chapter the reader is introduced to a series of problems related to the financial management of the hotel. This case study approach to learning is particularly useful as it enables realistic tasks to be carried out and analysed, allowing students to apply their theoretical knowledge to practical everyday problems. It thus develops their analytical and problem solving skills, and assists in developing their competences in financial management.

The Croeso Hotel and Leisure Complex

Sarah Darwin and Kate Jenkins

Sarah Darwin and Kate Jenkins first met five years ago when they both worked in Manchester for World Leisure, an international hotel and leisure group. Sarah left the organisation two years ago to take up an appointment as the General Manager of the Greenacres Country House Hotel in Somerset. Kate meanwhile remained at World Leisure as Marketing Director. Later that year Kate's husband died and as a result she was forced to review her circumstances as she had two children, Tom and Alice, to look after as a single parent. Kate had always kept in contact with Sarah and when she telephoned to tell her of her husband's death Sarah invited the family for a weekend at Greenacres.

During the weekend the women talked at length about Kate's problems and in particular their desire to work for themselves. Sarah felt she was at a crossroads in her life. She was a committed career woman and in her heart she had always wanted to run her own hotel.

As the two friends discussed their futures it became clear that by pooling their resources they could go into partnership and own their own business. Both had excellent qualifications and experience. Sarah had a Higher National Diploma in Hospitality Management and Kate had a degree in Leisure Management plus a Diploma in Marketing. Together they would make a formidable team.

Buying and refurbishing the hotel

Following her weekend at Greenacres Kate returned home to see her solicitor Mr Brooks-Wilson to discuss her future financial position. She found that life policies would mean that after repayment of the mortgage on the family home she would have £250,000 to invest, so she and the children would have no immediate financial worries. Now that Kate had the financial resources necessary to pursue her plans, she proceeded to sell her home and over the coming months she and Sarah began their search for a suitable hotel.

After carrying out initial enquiries about property prices it was agreed that North Wales would be the ideal location for their venture as Kate had been born in Dolgellau and had relatives and friends in the area. Sarah had always been a sports enthusiast and liked the idea of living near the mountains. Having viewed a number of properties the two women attended an auction where they were able to purchase the ideal property, together with many of the fixtures and fittings which were being sold off on behalf of the liquidator.

The Croeso Hotel had been built in the Victorian era and had 40 bedrooms. It had retained all its original elegance although it was in need of redecoration and refurbishment. The location was ideal, near the main road and yet standing in secluded grounds. The hotel cost £140,000 which included the furniture, fittings and equipment.

Having purchased the hotel Kate and Sarah set about organising the redecoration and refurbishment programme that was necessary. They had estimated that it would cost £40,000–£60,000 to redecorate all the bedrooms and public areas. The furniture, carpets and curtains were acceptable and it was agreed that these would be replaced at a later stage when the hotel was bringing in more revenue. It was essential that some of the kitchen equipment was replaced to meet safety and hygiene regulations. Having decided on the work that needed to be carried out in the immediate future Sarah contacted local builders and asked them for estimates. Within two weeks the painters were in the hotel and work was underway to restore the Croeso to its former glory.

The marketing plan and market research

While Sarah took charge of this project Kate began working on a marketing plan for the business. She identified **two** main market segments:

(1) Individuals wanting a restful holiday with good food and leisure activities.
(2) Groups who would wish to stay one or two nights at the hotel as part of a sightseeing tour package.

Pricing and tariff structure

An important part of the market research was analysing **local competitors** to assess their facilities, occupancy levels, guest profiles and pricing strategies. As a result of this exercise Kate proposed the following tariff structure:

Tariff per person per night, including VAT and full British breakfast:

	£
• Single room	52.50
• Standard double room	40.00
• Luxury double room	45.00
• Suite	62.50

	£
Luncheon, including VAT	10.95
Dinner, including VAT	21.00

Kate would be exploring the marketing opportunities of a flexible pricing structure in the future.

Advertising and launch

As part of the marketing strategy Kate worked with a designer to produce a colour brochure for the hotel. She also arranged for advertisements to appear in several British and European newspapers.

Six months from the day of buying the hotel the opening day was fast approaching. All the planning and hard work would now be tested by the market. To signify the opening of the hotel the two women held a champagne reception for local suppliers, business contacts and the press. Having successfully launched the hotel Sarah and Kate now face the challenge of running the business. Over the coming months and years they will have to make a range of financial decisions. These will unfold at the end of each chapter in the form of a set of Study Tasks which will build on the theory covered in each chapter. Suggested answers are found on pp. 242ff.

Acknowledgements

The authors acknowledge with thanks permission to use copyright material from Youngs Breweries plc for the Balance Sheet in Figure 6.5; and Cadbury Schweppes plc for the Profit and Loss Account and Balance Sheet in Figures 10.1 and 10.2.

Every effort has been made to trace all the copyright-holders, but if any have been inadvertently overlooked the publishers will be pleased to make the necessary arrangement at the first opportunity.

The authors also wish to thank John Winckler for all his help with the book, and Barbara Docherty and Keith Povey for editing the text.

We would also like to thank Andrea West at the University of Surrey for help with the typing, Tony Head for his advice and the academic staff at our universities for their many helpful comments and advice with this book.

SALLY MESSENGER
HUMPHREY SHAW

Part I
Understanding Financial Statements: Basic Principles

1 The Users of Financial Statements

The accounts of the business

Today's managers are fortunate in living in an age where they have at their disposal a wealth of financial information to help them make correct business decisions. Computerisation and other new technology has provided managers with the opportunity to receive a wide range of statements relating to the **performance** of the business. Whilst these reports can be extremely helpful it should be remembered that if information is to be useful it must be **relevant**, **reliable**, **complete**, **objective**, **timely**, **comparable** and **understandable** to the person receiving it. If it fails to meet these criteria it ceases to be usable information and is valueless to the manager.

All businesses must produce financial accounts which show **two** things:

> **(1)** The profits or losses made during the last financial year.
>
> **(2)** A statement which shows the property and other **assets** which the business has, together with the amount of money **financing** it. This money is referred to as the firm's **liabilities**, and will include share capital and loans.

These two accounting statements are referred to as the Profit and Loss account and the Balance Sheet.

These accounts are prepared for the **owners**. Outside parties must also be able to have access to this information if the business enjoys the privilege of limited liability, which means that the owners are not personally responsible, provided they have traded legally, for the debts of the business. There is a higher degree of risk in trading with such companies, and this is why they must publish their accounts, filing a copy at Companies House which may be read by the public. Sole traders and partnerships in general do not have limited liability and so their owners are responsible for the debts of the business. As a result they do not have to make their accounts public.

The users of financial information

As well as owners there are a number of other groups who are interested in the financial performance of an organisation. These include lenders, customers and the tax authorities. Much of the information these groups require will be contained in the final set of published accounts. The real problem is how to present this information to people who have a financial interest but who are not accountants or financial managers. This has been a problem for a number of years; in an attempt to solve it the Accounting Standards Steering Committee in 1974 looked into the aims and scope of published final accounts. Their report, published in 1975, was called *The Corporate Report*, and it set out **seven** separate user groups of financial information.

- Shareholders
- Lenders
- Employees
- Financial advisors
- Commercial parties
- Government
- The public

Shareholders

These are the people who own the company and have bought or subscribed for a share in the business. Their reward for investing in the company is a share of the profits which they receive in the form of a **dividend**. In order to make decisions about buying and selling shares shareholders need financial information. One problem facing an investor is that the information received will cover **past** trading activities, and this is not always a guarantee of **future** performance.

Lenders

There are few businesses which can raise all of the capital which they need just from shareholders and by reinvesting past profits. The additional money must therefore, be borrowed from banks or the capital markets. "Capital market" is the term used for any financial market where money can be borrowed or lent. Although lenders are not owners they nevertheless need information about the extent to which a firm can meet its **interest and capital repayments**.

Employees

Legally, an employee has no right to receive a set of financial accounts unless the employee is also a shareholder. Nevertheless most large companies are keen to publicise the financial position of the business by including important pieces of information in company newsletters or on notice boards. The financial strengths of any organisation inevitably determine the fortunes of its workforce. If profits are good wages should increase and profit-sharing schemes and other benefits may be introduced. If profits decline jobs and wages may fall, leading to financial hardship for those affected. As a result all employees are interested to some extent in the **profitability** of the business, even if they are not able to understand fully all of the information contained in a set of annual accounts.

Financial advisers

People such as stockbrokers and financial advisers make their living by advising clients how they should invest their savings. Before they can offer any advice they need information about the companies which they may recommend to investors. Financial advisers have the necessary skills to analyse and study a firm's accounts and make predictions on the future level of economic activity, which will have an impact on a firm's **earnings** and **cash flow**.

Commercial parties

The Corporate Report referred to customers, suppliers and business competitors as the "Business Contact Group". All of these parties need financial information. **Customers** may be reluctant to buy a firm's products if there has been a lot of bad publicity about the company's financial performance: most customers are unwilling to buy products from organisations who may not be able to honour guarantees in the future because they have ceased trading. **Suppliers** need to be certain that their customers are creditworthy and that invoices will be paid and contracts honoured. Any business which is unable to pay suppliers promptly soon finds it difficult to get additional credit, and its orders are generally not dealt with as fast as those firms who have good credit credentials, as we will see in Chapter 19. Finally **competitors** will want to know how other firms in the same industry are performing. The largest firm in an industry sector is often regarded as a barometer, and so other companies will wish to know if their performance is above or below the industry standard. This information is particularly valuable if management are considering a **takeover bid**, or **merging** their business interests with former competitors.

Government

The government raises a significant proportion of its revenue either directly or indirectly from business. With the exception of goods which are either exempt or zero rated for VAT purposes registered businesses must collect the tax from customers, as we will see in Chapter 9. The money is then paid to Customs and Excise who collect it on behalf of the government. The Inland Revenue similarly will collect employees' Pay As You Earn (PAYE) contributions and Corporation Tax is payable on company profits. If the correct **tax payments** are to be made accurate records must be kept of all financial transactions, and these must be available for inspection by the tax authorities if required.

In addition to these tax demands various government departments collect data from companies to assist them in monitoring and publishing **statistics** related to the economy. The Department of Employment collects information on employees' pay which is then used for calculating average wage rates in the economy, for example.

The Public

This was the final category of users defined in *The Corporate Report*. It made the point that businesses do not exist in a vacuum but are part of society and so must be able to answer society's questions. Not all of these questions will be financial but they are likely to have financial repercussions for many interested parties such as environmental and consumer groups who will often require information on, for example, the company's recycling policies and the costs and savings involved.

Making financial information accessible

For most people a set of company accounts are difficult to understand. Many firms try to make this task easier by using statistical presentation techniques, such as pie charts and bar charts to communicate the financial position of the business. Each user group will require different types of information, and this needs to be considered when preparing final accounts.

Study tasks

1 Identify the main groups of people who will be interested in the **financial performance** of the Croeso Hotel and Leisure Complex.

2 In order to ensure that everyone in the hotel is working towards the same goals Kate and Sarah have made a policy decision to keep their staff regularly informed about the financial performance of the business:

(a) Draw up a list of the **items of financial information** that you consider should be given to the staff, and give reasons for your choice.

(b) How **regularly** do you recommend that this information should be provided?

(c) Suggest ways in which this information could be **communicated**, and outline the advantages and disadvantages of each.

3 The Croeso Hotel has been asked if it would be prepared to sponsor a local charitable event. Sarah and Kate, together with a group of local businesspeople, will be meeting to discuss budgeted costs and revenue. They have already prepared figures on sales and costs for the hotel.

Budgeted sales and costs		
	£	£
Revenues		8,000
Sponsorship		2,000
Food	4,000	
Alcohol	3,500	
Prizes	500	
Wages	1,500	
Band	500	

Prepare a pie chart to display this information to delegates at the meeting. What are the advantages of presenting financial information in this format to a largely non-financially specialist audience?

4 Last week an article appeared in the local paper criticising the use of disposable products, and cited the catering industry as being particularly environmentally unfriendly. Sarah and Kate have asked you to advise them how they can develop policies to reassure guests and customers that the Croeso Hotel has a responsible attitude to the environment.

5 The Croeso Hotel is placing orders with suppliers, and some have asked for a credit reference. (a) What information will they require, and (b) who should Sarah and Kate ask for such a reference?

6 Sarah and Kate are aware that a wealth of financial information is available about the hotel and leisure industries but do not know where to find it. What information would be useful to their business? Briefly outline its sources.

2 Accounting Concepts and Conventions

Preparing the final accounts

When preparing final accounts the aim is to present a "true and fair view" of the financial position of the business. This statement has not yet been defined in any legislation or court case but is generally accepted to mean a "fair view" without bias. In order to achieve this accountants are required to base their work on a set of principles which are usually referred to as **concepts** and **conventions**. These principles are important for two reasons:

---

(1) If firms were allowed to change their accounting methods each year it would be difficult to **compare** one year's results with another
(2) It would be impossible to make **interfirm** comparisons.

The objective behind the accounting conventions is to standardise the **presentation** and **treatment** of financial information in final accounts. The rules relating to published accounts are referred to as the "regulatory framework". These regulations are very complicated and detailed and are currently the subject of debate as accountants, industrialists and academics discuss the best way of presenting this information. Although the framework is a study in itself it is sufficient for most users if they have an appreciation of the main accounting conventions.

In addition to these conventions there are the requirements of the Companies Acts, the requirements of the Stock Exchange for publicly quoted businesses and the Standard Statements of Accounting Practice, now replaced by the Financial Reporting Standards' as issued by the Accounting Standard's Board.

Accounting concepts and conventions

Business entity

The reasoning behind the business entity principle is that the private financial transactions of the **owners** must be kept separate from those of the **business**. This is the case be they a sole trader or a publicly quoted company. If an individual starts a business by withdrawing money from a savings account, this is recorded as an introduction of capital to the firm: in the firm's accounts no record is made of how it has affected the **individual's** wealth. All money provided by the owners is treated as a **liability**: in effect, it is the sum of money which the business **owes to the owners**.

Money measurement concept

A set of accounts only shows those items to which a **monetary value** can be attributed. As a result an effective management team and loyal workforce, although of great benefit to the business, will not appear in the final accounts as no monetary value can be placed on them.

This concept highlights the limitations of measuring a business in purely financial terms. During periods of high inflation there is the added danger that monetary values become distorted: inflation affects the value of a unit of currency by increasing the **price of assets** and reducing the **real value of debts**.

Duality

The principle of duality is based on the premise that every financial transaction has **two effects**: one showing the assets of the business and the other showing the money which is financing it. This is why assets always equal liabilities plus capital.

Going concern

It is a convention in accounting that a business will **continue** indefinitely unless there is an intention to the contrary. If the owner of a small enterprise intends to retire and liquidate the business it would be wrong to apply this concept; the accounts would state the owner's intention to sell, thereby showing that the business will not be a going concern for much longer.

It is for this reason that accountants choose to record the assets in the Balance Sheet at their **original cost price** and not at their current market value. This method is known as the "historical cost concept" and incorporates the going concern concept.

Prudence

In accounting, a sale is recorded when the goods are **sold**, not when the cash is actually **received** (see Realisation below). When a firm makes sales on credit it is owed money; there is therefore the possibility that some of these debtors **will not pay**. The prudence concept attempts to take account of any overstatement of the firm's financial position by requiring a provision to be made for any such possible **non-payment**.

Realisation

In accounting, income is treated as earned when a **sale is made** and an **invoice raised**, not when the cash is **received**.

Accruals

When a set of final accounts are prepared the aim is to balance one year's **income** with **expenditure**. Timing differences in the payment of bills will mean that at the financial year end some bills will remain unpaid whilst others (like insurance) will have been paid in advance. This necessitates the adding of any moneys still owing to the expenses side of the Profit and Loss Account and the deduction of any prepayments. Money owing must be shown as a liability and sums prepaid are treated as a short-term asset.

Consistency

It is essential that each year the **same method** is used for presenting financial information. If this were not done different results could be achieved, leading to a distortion of the firm's true financial position. Fixed assets such as buildings and equipment wear out with use; roofs need repairing and machines need updating, and these are the costs of using the assets. A charge to cover this cost must therefore be applied to the Profit and Loss Account. This is called **depreciation**. The aim is to charge a **set amount over the life of the asset**, thereby making a charge against profit for its use. If this did not happen the firm's profits would be overstated. The consistency concept ensures that users can compare one year's figures with another, knowing that they have been prepared in the same manner.

This concept does not, however, prohibit change if there is a good reason for it, but the **reason** and the **change** must both be disclosed in the accounts.

Materiality

Whenever a firm spends money it must be shown either as an **expense** in the Profit and Loss Account or as an **asset** in the Balance Sheet. If the expenditure has a life of less than 1 year it is regarded as **revenue expenditure** and is shown in the Profit and Loss Account: an example would be the the rent payable on using a building or employees' wages.

If the expenditure gives rise to a benefit which lasts longer than 1 year, such as the purchase of a freehold building, it is regarded as **capital expenditure**, and is shown in the Balance Sheet.

This distinction between revenue and capital expenditure is not always in practice clear cut: firms will have different policies. What a small firm may regard as capital expenditure a large one may treat as revenue. A large hotel may treat any purchase under £100 as revenue expenditure, whereas a small guest house would record it as capital expenditure.

The guiding principle should be that expenditure will not be treated as being capital should the **costs of depreciating** prove to be **excessive in relation to the asset's value**.

Legal requirements of the Companies Acts

The Companies Acts specify the legal requirements which must be met by companies when presenting their annual accounts. The information which must be disclosed, and the manner in which it is to be presented, is specified in the 1985 Companies Act. The accounts must be **audited** and must give a **true and fair view** of the state of the business. These legal requirements change from time to time to take account of **EC Directives**, and new developments which require legislation, such as the new concern about some companies' environmentally-unfriendly actions.

The requirements of the Stock Exchange

The aim of Stock Exchange requirements is to **protect investors** who wish to purchase the shares of publicly quoted companies. The rules are contained in what is referred to as the **Yellow Book**, and **four** of the main rules are:

(a) The company must have traded successfully for at least **3 years**

(b) There must be enough shares sold to investors to create a **free market** in the company's financial paper (see Chapter 19)

(c) The company must be able to earn a reasonable level of profit, which for practical purposes means that profits before tax must be in excess of **1 million pounds**

(d) The company must agree to comply with the rules of the Stock Exchange; this means that the firm must declare **6 monthly** or **interim** results.

Financial Reporting Standards (formerly Statements of Standard Accounting Practice)

The chartered accountancy bodies used to issue accounting standards which dealt with the treatment and presentation of financial information in final accounts. Over the years there was criticism that the standards did not always represent the views of industrialists and so the Accounting Standards Board was set up with a wider membership. To date they have issued three Financial Reporting Standards which have covered cash flow statements, treatment of group accounts and extraordinary items. In the future more Financial Reporting Standards will be issued to resolve any other accounting controversies that may arise.

Accounting as an evolving discipline

Accountancy is an evolving subject which has to take account of ever-changing trading conditions, the presentation of new financial information and new sources of finance. These developments are highlighted in the national press and in a book of this type it is impossible to cover all of the areas where there is currently debate. Nevertheless it is important to understand the main principles and to keep in touch with developments in this area in your reading of the financial and specialist accountancy press.

Study tasks

Sarah and Kate have just received their first annual Accounts. They have six queries, shown below, and have sought your advice as to how they should interpret the figures.

1   The Sales figure is higher than the amount of cash which we have actually received from customers. Why have the accountants not taken the cash received as the figure for Sales?

2   The Wedgwood ashtrays which cost £30 and the Royal Worcester vase which cost £40 have not been shown as assets in the Balance Sheet. Why have these items not been included under the heading Fixtures and Fittings?

3   The Notes to the Accounts state that the motor van has been depreciated using the straight line method. But the amount charged for depreciation is less than its fall in value. Next year, should we use a different method which will reflect the van's market value?

4   The Balance Sheet shows the money which we put into the business. It is our company, so why have they shown our money as a liability?

5   Our chef is one of the best in the county. I think he is worth £5,000 to the business and yet the Accounts don't reflect this at all. Why has this information not been shown in the Accounts?

6   The Profit and Loss Account shows that we have paid all our expenses and yet the hotel still owes some suppliers money. Why don't the Accounts show this?

3 Establishing a Financial Record Keeping System

The financial transactions of the business

Managers need to know all of the financial transactions which take place during each trading day. Information is needed about the:

> - Level of **sales**
> - Amount of **stock** purchased
> - Amount of **money** owed to suppliers
> - **Expenses** such as rent and rates.

Financial accounting

The aim of financial accounting is to record each of these transactions in such a way that it provides management with an **information system**. It is from these records that final accounts are prepared which summarise the firm's **trading position** for a given period of time.

Historical records show that from the early civilisations people have kept financial data in one form or another. Today's system dates back to the Italian merchants of the 15th century who devised a clear, concise and effective method of recording financial transactions.

Computerised or manual accounting system?

Organisations today have a choice of using either the traditional manual method of book keeping or alternatively using one of the many computer packages available on the market. There are **two** major benefits of using a computer system:

- **Routine paperwork** is eliminated with the result that less staff are required to maintain the system
- Calculations are carried out **speedily** and **accurately**.

Not all businesses need a computerised system to operate efficiently, and before embarking on the purchase of an accounting package management should clearly identify the **needs** of the organisation and establish the requirements of a financial recording system to meet these needs. For many small businesses a manual system is often suitable; once the business develops and the volume of work grows a computerised system becomes beneficial. But whether the financial record keeping system selected is manual or computerised, the principles on which it is based and operated are the same.

The record keeping cycle

Although keeping financial records is a logical exercise people who are new to the subject sometimes find the process confusing. This is because book keeping is like a jigsaw with a number of parts that need to be fitted together before the whole picture can be seen. Before looking at the detail, therefore, it may be helpful to present an overview of the system in the form of the diagram in Figure 3.1, showing the transactions of the Better Brew off-licence and their presentation in the accounts of the business.

Entering transactions in the Day Books (Step 1)

Day Books are also referred to as Books of Original Entry, Books of Prime Entry, Journals or Subsidiary Books of Account. As can be seen in Figure 3.1 there are a number of Day Books which can be used to record transactions which occur every day in the course of business. The decision regarding which book to enter the transaction in is based on the **nature of the event**, as demonstrated in Figure 3.2.

Figure 3.1 The Better Brew off-licence financial record keeping cycle

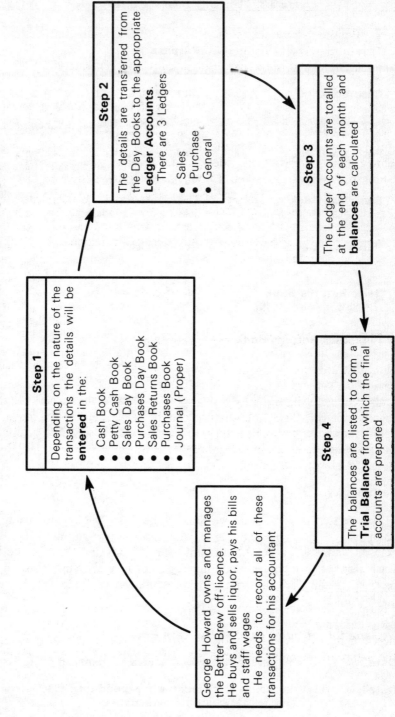

Step 1

Depending on the nature of the transactions the details will be **entered** in the:

- Cash Book
- Petty Cash Book
- Sales Day Book
- Purchases Day Book
- Sales Returns Book
- Purchases Book
- Journal (Proper)

Step 2

The details are transferred from the Day Books to the appropriate **Ledger Accounts**.

There are 3 Ledgers

- Sales
- Purchase
- General

Step 3

The Ledger Accounts are totalled at the end of each month and **balances** are calculated

Step 4

The balances are listed to form a **Trial Balance** from which the final accounts are prepared

George Howard owns and manages the Better Brew off-licence.
He buys and sells liquor, pays his bills and staff wages
He needs to record all of these transactions for his accountant

Figure 3.2   The Day Books: entries made

Title	Purpose
Cash Book	Although the word "cash" appears in the title of this Day Book it actually records both cash and cheque payments and receipts
Petty Cash Book	Small amounts of cash payments are recorded, such as the purchase of stamps or taxi fares
Sales Day Book	This book records, in date order, the sale of any goods sold on credit to customers
Purchases Day Book	Goods which are bought for re-sale on credit from suppliers are entered in date order in this book
Sales Returns Book (Returns Inwards Book)	Where customers return goods which are unacceptable to them, the details are entered in this book.
Purchases Returns Book (Returns Outwards Book)	If after purchasing goods they are returned to the supplier because they do not meet requirements, the details are recorded in this book
Journal (Proper)	Any other transactions such as correction of errors in the Ledger Accounts are entered in this Day Book

Cash Book

There are two possible presentations of the Cash Book – one using **two** columns and the other using **three** columns. The two-column Cash Book contains details of all cash and bank transactions and the three-column Cash Book also includes a column for recording **discounts** allowed and received. Figure 3.3 illustrates the presentation of these details in the Cash Book.

Explanation of terms used in the Cash Book

Date   This is the day the money was **received** or **paid out** of the business

Details   This a description of the **income** or **expenditure**; where names are used, these refer to **customer** or **supplier**

Figure 3.3 Layout of a three-column Cash Book

Debit

Date	Details	Folio	Discount	Cash	Bank
Sep 1	Balance	b/d		320	9,080
Sep 3	Burns	SL9	20		260
Sep 9	Jones	SL15			80

Credit

Date	Details	Folio	Discount	Cash	Bank
2	Jones	PL4	5	45	
6	Wages	GL			340

Folio   This section contains a **reference code** which represents the other half to the double entry of the transaction; the Sales Ledger is represented by SL, the Purchase Ledger by PL, and the General Ledger by GL, followed by the **page number** on which the entry details can be found.

Discount   This only appears in the three-column Cash Book
               Cash discount is often given to customers who settle their accounts promptly; discount is likewise received from suppliers for the same reason – the former is referred to as **discounts allowed** and the latter is called **discounts received**
               Accountants never record trade discount as a separate item.
               Where money is received or **paid out**, it is entered in this column

Bank   Payments **made** or **received** by **cheque** are entered in this column
               At the end of each month the cash book is **totalled** and **balanced** (see Chapter 4)

Petty Cash Book

In any business there will be daily expenditure of small amounts of money to cover miscellaneous items. In order to group these relatively small payments together a Petty Cash Book is used by most firms. A member of staff is often made responsible for managing the Petty Cash Book and they usually use the **Imprest System**. This system provides the petty cashier with a sum of money from which payments are paid out. At the end of the month the expenditure is totalled and checked. The amount spent is then reimbursed to the petty cashier for the beginning of the next month's payments. Figure 3.4 shows the layout of a typical Petty Cash Book.

Explanation of terms used in the Petty Cash Book

Receipts   The sum of money given to the petty cashier to **pay out** for miscellaneous items

Folio   The **double entry reference** – in this example CB represents "Cash Book"

Date   The **day** on which the money was **paid out**

Details   Items for which money was paid out

Voucher No When the items are paid for, the amount is recorded on a **voucher**

Total   The sum **paid out** for each item

Analysis   These identify how much has been spent on **each item**

Columns   There can be as many analysis columns as are required by the organisation

Figure 3.4 Presentation of the Petty Cash Book

Receipts	Folio	Date	Details	Vouch. No.	Total	Travel	Postage	Stationery	Ledger Folio	Ledger Accs
£100.00	CB7	Jun 1	Cash	–						
		Jun 2	Stamps	1	£2.60		£2.60			
		Jun 4	Taxi	2	£3.50	£3.50				
		Jun 5	Envelopes	3	£1.70			£1.70		
		Jun 6	Pens	4	£5.80			£5.80		
					£13.60	£3.50	£2.60	£7.50		
					GL17	GL5	GL15	GL13		
£13.60	CB 8	Jun 6 Jun 6	Cash Balance	c/d	100.00 £113.60					
£113.60										
£100.00		Jun 7	Balance	b/d						

Purchases Day Book

The majority of businesses **buy** most of their goods and services **on credit**. In order to record how much has been bought form different suppliers the details of the credit purchases are entered in the Purchases Day Book. This contains a listing, in date order, of the **suppliers** to whom **money is owed** together with the invoice number, reference number showing where the entry appears in the Purchases Ledger (which is explained in Chapter 4) and the amount of money to be paid. Look at Figure 3.5.

Figure 3.5   Purchases Day Book: entries made

Date	Supplier	Invoice No.	Folio	£
Jan 1	P. Bleeze	8/241	PL 5	520
Jan 9	S. Lord	2/021	PL 11	780
Jan 13	E. Bains	3/908	PL 4	220
Jan 17	F. Franklin	4/501	PL 7	109
Jan 23	Y. Norman	9/981	PL 9	61
Jan 31	U. Denby	6/241	PL 6	25
Transferred to Purchases Account			GL 42	£1,715

As can be seen, the Purchases Day Book provides a summary of how much has been supplied on credit. At the end of each month the Day Book is totalled and the amount is transferred to the Purchases Account.

Sales Day Book

As well as buying goods on credit, businesses often **sell** to customers **on credit**. Indeed, to remain in a competitive position it is often very important that they allow their customers this facility. When items are sold on credit a similar procedure is followed to that used when purchasing goods in this way. The sales are entered in what is known as the Sales Day Book. When the goods are sold, an **invoice** is produced and sent to the purchaser which details the date, the name of the buyer, the invoice number, the reference number in the Sales Ledger and the amount due. Look at Figure 3.6.

Figure 3.6   Sales Day Book: entries made

Date	Customer	Invoice No.	Folio	£
Jan 5	Z. Nolze	20/980	SL 64	635
Jan 19	H. Patel	20/981	SL 67	490
Jan 22	J. Logie	20/982	SL 63	988
Jan 31	R. Farnham	20/983	SL 60	854
Transferred to Sales Account			GL 51	£2,967

The Sales Day Book contains a detailed listing of how much of the business has been on credit. At the end of each month, the entries are totalled and transferred to the Sales Account.

Returns

During the course of trade, goods very often have to be **returned** either because they do not meet the specification or because there has been a mistake and the wrong goods have been delivered. Whether a business is returning goods to suppliers, or alternatively receiving returned items from customers, it needs to **record the returns** so that the necessary adjustments can be carried out when the accounts are drawn up. If a business sells £55,000 worth of goods and £2,000 worth are returned, the £2,000 must be deducted to reflect the correct sales total for the business. A similar calculation should be carried out when purchases are returned to a supplier.

When goods are returned by customers a **credit note** is issued to them. This note confirms that the customer has been allowed the value of the goods and that their account has been credited with the amount. The details stated on the credit note are also entered in the Sales Returns Book.

Figure 3.7   Sales Returns Book: entries made

Date	Customer	Credit Note No.	Folio	£
Jan 10	Z. Nolze	41/630	SL 64	30
Jan 29	J. Logie	41/631	SL 63	120
Transferred to Returns Inwards Account			GL 93	150

In the same way, when a business returns goods to a supplier a **debit note** is sent stating the amount of money the firm expects to receive for the faulty or incorrect items. This means that the personal account of the supplier is debited for this amount – the debit note is sent to the supplier to inform them of the adjustment. The details of all debit notes sent to suppliers are entered in the Purchases Returns Book. Look at Figure 3.8.

Figure 3.8   Purchases Returns Book: entries made

Date	Supplier	Debit Note No.	Folio	£
Jan 15	E. Bains	57/241	PL 4	46
Jan 20	F. Franklin	57/242	PL 7	34
Transferred to Returns Outwards Account			GL 95	80

Preparing the Ledger Accounts (Step 2)

Having completed Step 1, we now move to Step 2, which is concerned with transferring details from the Day Books to the appropriate Ledger Accounts. It is at this point that the **principle of double entry book keeping** has to be followed, as Chapter 4 demonstrates.

Study tasks

1 Sarah and Kate are establishing a record keeping system for the Croeso Hotel. Advise them on Day Books in which the following transactions should be entered:

   (a) The purchase on credit from Simon Bloom of £35 in green-grocery
   (b) The payment of £2.80 cash for a taxi fare for a member of staff
   (c) The payment of £129 cash to Reg Blair, the plumber for maintenance work carried out
   (d) The receipt of £500 cash from Philip Liley, a local businessman, for a conference booking
   (e) Returning £40 of meat to Frank Harwood, the butcher
   (f) The sale of two weeks' accommodation on credit to Wrights Consultants

(**g**) Providing a refund of one night's accommodation to Audrey Donaldson.

2   From the following details of hotel transactions provide Kate and Sarah with an extract of the Cash Book showing how these entries should be written up:

Mar		£
1	Opening balance	150
2	Postage	12
3	Cash sales	30
4	Rent	18
5	Wages	25
6	Petrol	10
7	Cash sales	60
8	Paid cash into bank	80

3   Sarah and Kate have made a number of small payments for miscellaneous items.
    You have been asked to enter the following items in the Petty Cash Book for them:

May		£
1	Cash Receipt	100.00
2	Taxi Fare	1.60
3	Envelopes	2.30
4	Taxi fare	5.40
5	Pencils	1.90
6.	Flowers	9.80
7	Paper	2.40
8.	Taxi Fare	3.80

4 From the following details of transactions at the hotel prepare a:

(**a**) Purchases Day Book
(**b**) Sales Day Book.

Sep

1   Bought fresh fish on account from Jones and Sons for £48

2   D & A Brothers held a two-day exhibition of their china and glass products in the hotel, the bill came to £274 and was put on the firm's account

3   A wine order was supplied to the hotel by Peter Bright at a cost of £318, this was put on the hotel's account

5   Mr and Mrs Sandhurst stayed for one week in the hotel and asked for the bill of £882 to be put on their account

7   Sarah visited David Morris the local baker to collect a wedding cake he had prepared for them, the bill of £75 was put on the hotel's account

8   The local Business Club held a lunch at the hotel and asked the bill of £540 to be put on their account

11   Kate purchased a new line of shortbread biscuits from a sales representative from Hillars and asked them to place the order of £54 on account for the hotel

12   Mr Brian Walters stayed in the hotel one night and asked for his account of £69 to be sent to his company, Excel Computers.

15   Miss June Kelly held her 18th birthday party in the hotel and asked the hotel to send the account for £485 to her father, Mr Harold Kelly

16   Kate purchased some after-dinner mints from a new supplier, Specialities, for £32 and asked to put the bill on the hotel's account.

5 From the following information prepare a:

(**a**) Sales Returns Book
(**b**) Purchases Returns Book.

Sep

7 Received a cheque and letter from D&A Brothers querying the bill of £274 for their two-day exhibition; Kate looked into the matter and decided to return £25 to maintain goodwill

7 Kate refused to pay the bill of £318 to Peter Bright because the wine had not been up to standard; after speaking on the phone she received a credit note for £50 from Peter Bright

15 Sarah received a letter of complaint from the Chairman of the Business Club, informing her that three people had suffered food poisoning after they had eaten lunch at the hotel on 8 September. Sarah was very worried about bad publicity and she immediately sent a £75 cheque to the Chairman for the three guests who had been ill

19 Having purchased the new dinner mints from Specialities, Kate opened the first box to find the chocolates had a bloom on them; she immediately contacted the Sales Representative she had dealt with and he promised that a credit note for £10 would be put in the post to her that evening.

---

6 When examining the Day Books and Cash Books for the business, Sarah and Kate have experienced some difficulties understanding one or two of the terms used. Prepare a memo for them answering their three queries:

(**a**) What is the difference between trade discount and cash discount?

(**b**) When must we use the Petty Cash Book instead of the Cash Book for items of expenditure?

(**c**) Why do we have to keep Sales Returns and Purchases Returns Day Books? Why can we not just carry out the deductions for goods returned in the Sales or Purchases Day Books?

4 Preparing the Ledger Accounts

Double entry book keeping

The principle of double entry book keeping hinges on the fact that there are **two parts** to all financial transactions. If an off-licence purchases champagne they acquire a stock of champagne, but at the same time they have to pay for it, which means they have **less cash** as a result. In the same way when they sell the champagne they will reduce their stocks but they will receive cash. With financial transactions which do not include credit the firm is exchanging its cash either to acquire new assets or to pay expenses. The transactions of Jumps, Memories and Snack on Wheels illustrate the principles involved.

The double entry principle

(**1**) Jumps, a keep fit club, has purchased 10 new work-out mats for use in its gym. The total cost of the mats is £200 cash. The effect of this purchase on the accounts is:

- The **assets** of Jumps are **increased by £200**
- The **cash** held by the company is **reduced by £200**

(**2**) Memories, a tourist gift shop, sells 40 key rings a week in the height of the season. Each key ring is priced at £1.50 and the total revenue received is £60 cash per week. The effect of these sales on the accounts is:

- The **stock** held by Memories is **decreased to the value of £60**
- The shop has **£60 in cash from the sales**

(**3**) Snack on Wheels purchases a new motorbike to deliver lunchtime sandwich and food items to customers working in offices around the City of London. The motorbike cost £5,250 and was purchased by cheque. The effect of this purchase on the accounts is:

- The **assets** of the business are **increased by £5,250**
- The firm's **bank deposit** is **reduced by £5,250.**

Recording transactions in the Ledger Accounts (Step 2)

As every financial transaction has two parts it means that **two ledger accounts** have to be opened. The basic principle of the double entry system is that each financial transaction is recorded twice – one as a **debit** entry and once as a **credit** entry. In accounting, the word "debit" means "left" and "credit" means "right". These words refer to the **side of the ledger** on which the entries must be recorded.

The Italian merchants in the 15th century decided that an **increase** in an asset such as the firm gaining more cash would be entered on the debit side. A **decrease** in an asset such as spending cash must, therefore, be recorded on the **credit** side.

We can now demonstrate how the three transactions shown on p. 28 should be recorded in the Ledger Accounts. (Note that Ledger Accounts are often referred to as "T" Accounts because of their presentation.)

(1) Jumps

The two accounts affected by the purchase of the work-out mats are:

- Equipment Account
- Cash Account

As the keep fit club is acquiring more equipment, this account must be **debited**. The Cash Account is therefore **credited**.

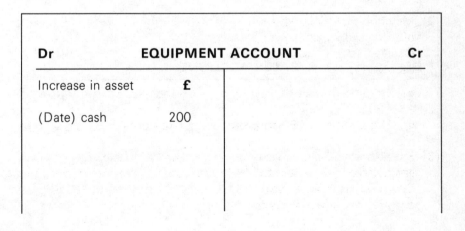

Dr	EQUIPMENT ACCOUNT		Cr
Increase in asset	£		
(Date) cash	200		

Dr	CASH ACCOUNT		Cr
	Decrease in asset	£	
	(Date) Jumps	200	

(2) Memories

The two accounts affected by the sale of the key rings are:

- Cash Account
- Sales Account

As the Cash Account is receiving **more money** this account must be **debited**. The Sales Account is therefore **credited**.

Dr	CASH ACCOUNT		Cr
Increase in asset	£		
Date Sales	60		

Dr	SALES ACCOUNT		Cr
	Increase in income	£	
	(Date) Cash	60	

(3) Snack on Wheels

The two accounts affected by the purchase of the new motorbike are:

- Motor Vehicles Account
- Cash Account

As the Motor Vehicles Account is **acquiring** a motorbike the account must be **debited**. The bank column of the Cash Account is therefore **credited**.

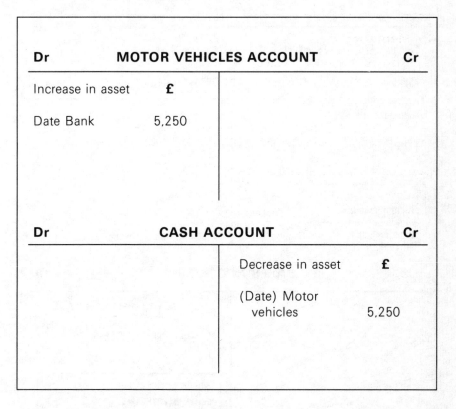

Dr	MOTOR VEHICLES ACCOUNT		Cr
Increase in asset	£		
Date Bank	5,250		

Dr	CASH ACCOUNT		Cr
		Decrease in asset	£
		(Date) Motor vehicles	5,250

Buying and selling on credit

So far, we have not considered any credit transactions. When a firm buys or sells on credit the Ledger Accounts must show how much is **owed** and **to whom**, plus what is **owed to the firm**.

If a business sells goods on credit the person buying the goods is called a **debtor** and is treated as an **asset** of the business. No money has changed hands and so the Ledger must show what was sold and the amount owed.

This is done by debiting the Debtor's Account and crediting the Sales Account.

The Swiss House Patisserie and the Aylmer Coffee House: credit purchases and sales

The Swiss House Patisserie has just sold £200 worth of gateaux and chocolates to the Aylmer Coffee House. To record this transaction, **debit** the Coffee House £200 and **credit** the Sales Account £200:

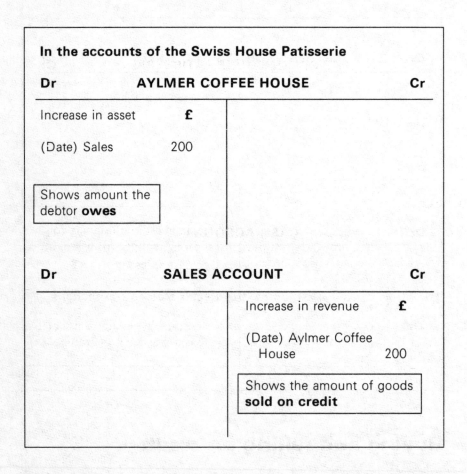

In the accounts of the Swiss House Patisserie

Dr	AYLMER COFFEE HOUSE		Cr
Increase in asset	£		
(Date) Sales	200		

Shows amount the debtor **owes**

Dr	SALES ACCOUNT		Cr
		Increase in revenue	£
		(Date) Aylmer Coffee House	200

Shows the amount of goods **sold on credit**

This involves buying goods on credit. In such cases the firm **gains** the **benefit** and at the same time **incurs** a **liability**. In the accounts whatever has been bought is recorded as a debit entry and the amount owing as a credit entry.

Now look at how the transaction can be recorded in the accounts of the Aylmer Coffee House:

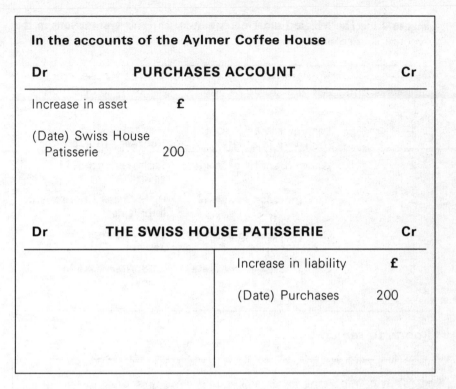

In the accounts of the Aylmer Coffee House

Dr	PURCHASES ACCOUNT		Cr
Increase in asset	£		
(Date) Swiss House Patisserie	200		

Dr	THE SWISS HOUSE PATISSERIE		Cr
		Increase in liability	£
		(Date) Purchases	200

As the system of double entry book keeping becomes familiar you will find it easy to know what is **owed** or is **owing**, simply from looking at which side the entry is recorded on.

The Magic Lantern Restaurant: the week's trading transactions

The manager of the Magic Lantern Restaurant has made a list of five financial transactions which have occurred in one week of trading:

1   Purchased food for £250 on credit from Hot 'N Spicy Wholesalers

2   Paid £875 wages in cash

3   Bought a van for £3,900 on credit from RightWheels

4   Paid £112 gas bill in cash

5   Restaurant cash sales £513.

The accounts in which these transactions have to be entered are:

Figure 4.1   The Magic Lantern Restaurant: entering transactions in the accounts

Transaction No.	Account to be Debited	Account to be Credited
1	Food purchases (**increase in assets**)	Hot 'N Spicy wholesalers (**increase in liabilities**)
2	Wages (**benefit of wages**)	Cash (**reduction in assets**)
3	Van (**increase in assets**)	RightWheels (**increase in liabilities**)
4	Gas (**increase in expense**)	Cash (**decrease in assets**)
5	Cash (**increase in assets**)	Sales (**decrease in stock**)

Points to remember

(a) It is important to remember that sales and any other income earned is always a **credit** entry

(b) It is correct to distinguish between an expense and the purchase of an asset; from the point of recording them in the ledgers, however, they are both dealt with in the same way: an increase in assets or the payment of an expense is always a **debit** item

(c) Whenever goods are sold on credit the person buying them will be shown as a **debit** entry

(d) Any goods bought on **credit** are shown as a credit entry from the supplier.

Accounts Ledgers in use

Within the double entry system of accounting there are a wide variety of accounts. These accounts are kept in one of three ledgers:

- **Sales or Debtors Ledger**
  In this ledger are all the **personal accounts** of individual customers or clients who have been sold goods or services **on credit** by the business

- **Purchases, Creditors or Bought Ledger**
  In this ledger are all the **personal accounts** of individual suppliers whom the business has purchased goods from **on credit**

- **General or Nominal Ledger**
  In this ledger are all the **impersonal accounts** of the business. Accountants sub-divide these into Real and Nominal Accounts: tangible items such as equipment, stock or vehicles are referred to as **Real Accounts** and items of day-to-day revenue and expenditure such as sales and purchases are referred to as **Nominal Accounts**.

For the Magic Lantern Restaurant, we can see its transactions listed in the appropriate ledgers in Figure 4.2 (on following page).

The majority of the accounts for the Magic Lantern Restaurant are in the General Ledger because they are concerned with day-to-day income and expenditure. Only one transaction appears in the Purchases Ledger because it is the only item of credit expenditure on goods for re-sale to customers. Whilst the purchase of the van is on credit also, it has been bought for use in the running of the restaurant and is therefore classified as a Real Account which will be assigned to the **General Ledger**.

Presentation of Ledger Accounts

In the past a ledger would take the form of a very large book in which were contained all the different accounts. Whilst this system is still used by a number of firms in some it will have been replaced by the computer. Where a computer system is in place it is possible to call up on the screen each ledger and its associated accounts. Whatever the system, the account should appear in the format shown in Figure 4.3 (on following page).

Each Ledger Account is only concerned with one kind of transaction, e.g. electricity, gas, advertising, wages, purchases, sales, rent. As most firms have a large number of transactions, a significant number of **individual accounts** have to be kept.

Figure 4.2 The Magic Lantern Restaurant: entering transactions in the Ledger

Transaction Number	Account to be Credited	Ledger	Account to be Debited	Ledger
1	Hot 'N Spicy Wholesalers	PL	Food purchases	GL
2	Cash	GL	Wages	GL
3	RightWheels	GL	Van	GL
4	Cash	GL	Gas	GL
5	Sales	GL	Cash	GL

Figure 4.3 Ledger Account format

(Debit) Dr   (Credit) Cr

Date	Details	Folio	£ p	Date	Details	Folio (Reference)	£ p

Explanation of terms used in the Ledger Accounts

Date	The day on which the transaction **occurred**
Details	Information about the transaction – in the Electricity Account details would be entered about **payments**, whether they were cash or cheque, for example.
Folio	This is the reference number which can be used to identify the **double entry** of the transaction
£ p	The amount **spent** or **received**.

Remember that these Ledger Accounts will be in the "T" Account format as we saw above:

Dr   **ADVERTISING**   **Cr**

Balancing Accounts (Step 3)

At the end of each month (usually) the **individual accounts** are balanced. To calculate the balance figure, the debit side of the account concerned is totalled and the credit side is also added up. The difference between the two sides is referred to as the "balance". The closing balance of one month becomes the **opening** balance of the next, as shown in Figure 4.4. (on the following page)

Preparing a Trial Balance (Step 4)

When all items of income and expenditure have been entered in the accounts following the double entry principle of book keeping, a **Trial Balance** is prepared. This is a listing of all the credit and debit account balances, which are then totalled in order to check that the two sums **agree**. If the two columns do agree it is a strong indication that the individual accounts have been prepared correctly, but is **not a guarantee**.

Figure 4.4   How to calculate the balance

Dr	CASH ACCOUNT				Cr
		£			**£**
Jan 1	Capital	10,000	Jan 1	Purchases	600
Jan 12	Sales	560	Jan 3	Rent	850
Jan 28	Sales	420	Jan 4	Advertising	120
			Jan 15	Wages	230
			Jan 23	Electricity	109
			Jan 31	Stationery	51
			Jan 31	Balance	9,020
		10,980			10,980
Feb 1 Opening balance 9,020					

There are a number of errors which are not necessarily revealed in the production of the Trial Balance:

- **Errors of omission**: Where a transaction has been **completely omitted** from the accounts

- **Compensating errors**: Where two errors are made that **cancel each other out**

- **Errors of principle**: Where an item is recorded in the **wrong type** of account

- **Errors of original entry**: Where the wrong figure is entered at the **beginning** and used thereafter

- **Errors of commission**: Where the correct figure is entered, but in the **wrong individual's** account

- **Reversal of entries**: Where a **credit** entry is incorrectly recorded as a **debit** entry, and vice versa, in the right accounts.

If the two columns **do not add up to the same figure**, one or more of the following reasons may be the cause:

- Incorrect **addition** of the debit and credit columns of the Trial Balance
- A **debit** balance on one account being entered in error on the **credit** side of the trial balance, and vice versa
- Incorrectly recording the **amount** of a **balance in the Trial Balance**
- Incorrectly calculating the **balance on a Ledger Account**
- Not completing the **double entry** for a transaction
- Recording a transaction **twice** as a credit entry or a debit entry
- Putting **two debits** or **two credits** for one transaction in the Ledger Accounts.

Figure 4.5 shows a typical Trial Balance for Trackers, an adventure holidays company.

Figure 4.5   Trackers: Trial Balance

	Dr £	Cr £
Capital		17,170
Cash	1,980	
Purchases	500	
Petrol	100	
Creditors		100
Debtors	2,000	
Vans	12,500	
Sales		250
Electricity	70	
Wages	230	
Rent	140	
	17,520	17,520

After the Trial Balance has been prepared the next stage is to prepare the final accounts, which consist of the Trading Profit and Loss account and the Balance Sheet (see Chapter 5).

Barbara Bloom: Posting enquiries and preparing a Trial Balance

Barbara Bloom has her own small party catering business which she has been running for the past 12 months. The following are the entries which were made in the accounts during her first month of trading;

Transactions for first month	£
1 Began the business with cash	3,750
2 Purchased a van for	950
4 Bought petrol	20
15 Purchased food for cash from Fresh Foods	180
17 Purchased wine	54
25 Catered for first customer S. Peabody and invoiced for	345
28 Paid for hire of catering equipment	37

Barbara Bloom's accounts now show the following.

Dr		CAPITAL ACCOUNT		Cr
	£			£
31 Balance	3,750	Cash		3,750
	3,750			3,750

Dr		CASH ACCOUNT		Cr
	£			£
1 Capital	3,750	2 Van		950
17 Sales	345	4 Petrol		20
		15 Food		180
		17 Wine		54
		28 Hire of catering equipment		37
		31 Balance		2,854
	4,095			4,095
1st Balance (start of next month)	2,854			

Dr		VAN ACCOUNT		Cr
		£		£
2	Cash	950	2 Balance	950
		950		950

Dr		PETROL ACCOUNT		Cr
		£		£
4	Cash	20	31 Balance	20
		20		20

Dr		FOOD PURCHASES ACCOUNT		Cr
		£		£
15	Cash	180	31 Balance	180
		180		180

Dr		WINE PURCHASES ACCOUNT		Cr
		£		£
17	Cash	54	31 Balance	54
		54		54

Dr		SALES ACCOUNT		Cr
		£		£
31	Balance	345	25 S. Peabody	345
		345		345

D_r	EQUIPMENT HIRE ACCOUNT			Cr
		£		£
25 Cash		37	31 Balance	37
		37		37

Barbara Bloom can now draw up the Trial Balance for the first month's trading, as in Figure 4.6.

Figure 4.6   Barbara Bloom: trading Trial Balance for first month

	Dr £	Cr £
Capital		3,750
Cash	2,854	
Food purchases	180	
Wine purchases	54	
Sales		345
Equipment Hire	37	
Van	950	
Petrol	20	
	4,095	4,095

Control Accounts

As we have seen, the Trial Balance is a listing of the debit and credit balances of accounts kept within the General Ledger. Within the Purchases and Sales Ledgers are kept all the personal accounts of suppliers from whom goods have been bought on credit or to whom goods have been sold on credit. Rather than list the balances of all the individual personal accounts in the Trial Balance **Control Accounts** are prepared for the Purchases and Sales Ledgers.

The Purchases Ledger Control Account and the Sales Ledger Control Account are not part of the double entry process – like the Trial Balance they serve only as a check on the arithmetic of the entries. Figures 4.7 and 4.8 show the items which will appear in the Purchase Ledger Control Account and the Sales Ledger Control Account.

Figure 4.7   Items which will appear in the Purchase Ledger Control Account

Dr	Cr
Total returns	Total balances b/d
Total cash	Total credit purchases
Total discounts received	Interest on overdue
Bills of Exchange payable	accounts
Sales ledger contras	
Total balances c/d	
————	————
	Total balances b/d

Figure 4.8   Items which will appear in the Sales Ledger Control Account

Dr	Cr
Total balances	Total returns
Total sales	Total cash
Dishonoured cheques	Total discounts allowed
Interest on overdue accounts	Total bad debts
	Bills of Exchange receivable
	Purchase Ledger contras
	Total Balances c/d
————	————
	Total balances b/d

Explanation of terms used in the Control Accounts

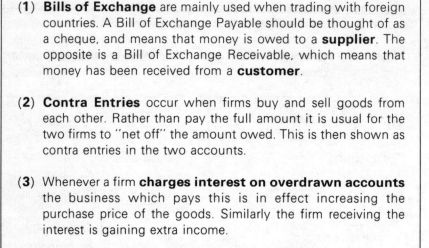

(1) **Bills of Exchange** are mainly used when trading with foreign countries. A Bill of Exchange Payable should be thought of as a cheque, and means that money is owed to a **supplier**. The opposite is a Bill of Exchange Receivable, which means that money has been received from a **customer**.

(2) **Contra Entries** occur when firms buy and sell goods from each other. Rather than pay the full amount it is usual for the two firms to "net off" the amount owed. This is then shown as contra entries in the two accounts.

(3) Whenever a firm **charges interest on overdrawn accounts** the business which pays this is in effect increasing the purchase price of the goods. Similarly the firm receiving the interest is gaining extra income.

As can be seen the Control Accounts are prepared using information from the Day Book, Cash Book and General Ledger. The Balances on the two Control Accounts are shown in the Trial Balance as **creditors** and **debtors**.

After the Trial Balance has been prepared the next stage is to prepare the final accounts which consist of the Trading and Profit and Loss Account and the Balance Sheet (see Chapters 5 and 6).

Importance of up-to-date and accurate financial record keeping

This Chapter has presented Steps 2–4 that have to be completed when maintaining a financial record keeping system. Once the principles of the process are understood the system is relatively easy to operate. There is a considerable amount of detailed work attached to book keeping and it forms the basis on which the final accounts are prepared and management decisions are taken. It is therefore, important that the accounts are kept **up to date** and are **accurate**.

Study tasks

1 For each of the following transactions of the Croeso Hotel identify which accounts should be **debited**, and which should be **credited**:

Transaction	Debit	Credit
(a) Opened company bank account with £1,000 cash		
(b) Received cheque for £50 from R. Green		
(c) Bought wine for £200 cash		
(d) Withdrew cash from the business £100		
(e) Bought petrol for £20 cash		
(f) Paid rates of £400 by cheque		

2 State whether the **opening balance** in the following Ledger Accounts should be recorded as a **debit** or a **credit** entry.

(**a**) Bank loan
(**b**) Discount allowed
(**c**) Sales
(**d**) Purchases
(**e**) Cash
(**f**) Discount received
(**g**) Petrol
(**h**) Fixtures and fittings
(**i**) Debtors
(**j**) Creditors.

3 Record the following transactions in the appropriate "T" Accounts for the Croeso Hotel:

Day

1 Withdrew £300 cash from company bank account

2 Spent £50 cash on motor repairs

3 Received £100 cash from customer
Paid £70 cash into bank account

4 Paid wages for cleaners £200 cash
Paid newsagent £60 cash

5 Withdrew £50 cash from bank
Bought £50 meat for cash.

---

4 Record the following transactions in the appropriate "T" Accounts for the Croeso Hotel:

Day

1 Bought £100 fish from SeaWorld on credit

2 Provided a dinner and dance for the local tennis club on account for £435

3 Bought new bar stools for £300 from Archers on credit

4 paid £100 cheque to SeaWorld

5 Received £500 cheque form the Mini Computer company.

---

5 In a Trial Balance, would the following balances appear as **debits** or as **credits**?

(a)	Sales	**(i)**	Equipment
(b)	Premises	**(j)**	Purchases
(c)	Drawings	**(k)**	Carriage outwards
(d)	Carriage inwards	**(l)**	Furniture
(e)	Debtors	**(m)**	Light and heat
(f)	Bank loan	**(n)**	Wages
(g)	Capital	**(o)**	Cash
(h)	Returns inwards	**(p)**	Insurance

---

6 From the following information draw up the Croeso Hotel's Trial Balance and calculate its capital:

	£
Wages	1,500
Heat and light	2,000
Carriage inwards	400
Cleaning	1,200
Rates	900
Discount received	400
Creditors	3,000
Motor expenses	1,000

5 Preparing a Trading and Profit and Loss Account

What profit has the business made?

Every business person will want to know the **profits** that their organisation has generated. In order to establish this accounts must be prepared which **summarise the trading** that has taken place during the last financial year. The owners and managers will not be the only people requiring this information. The tax authorities, outside lenders and investors will all want to know the profits made throughout the year, and the assets and liabilities of the business.

Stages in preparing the Profit and Loss Account

It is helpful to think of preparing a Profit and Loss Account as **two separate, but related**, stages.

Stage 1: the Trading Account

This will show the profit earned before the firm pays any expenses and is called the **gross profit**. It shows stock movements during the year, and from this can be calculated how much the business paid for the goods which it sold. By subtracting the cost of goods sold from the sales figure, the gross profit can be calculated.

Stage 2: the Profit and Loss Account

This illustrates the profit remaining after all expenses incurred in running the business are paid, which is called the **net profit**.

Information shown in the Trading and Profit and Loss Account

This statement summarises the firm's trading activities during the previous financial year. Although it is generally drawn up annually it can be produced more frequently if management want to know the firm's financial position at any particular date – they may wish to check whether the profits they are achieving match the **budgeted** figures, for example.

The Trading Account shows how much gross profit has been made, by deducting the cost of goods sold from the sales revenue. In essence the gross profit is the total of all the **individual profits** made on selling the organisation's goods and services.

Calculating Gross Profit

The Golf Shop: closing and opening stock

If all the goods bought for re-sale were sold within the financial year the gross profit would be calculated by simply deducting the cost of goods sold from the total sales. This would be entered in the accounts as shown in Figure 5.1.

Figure 5.1 The Golf Shop: Trading Account for the year ended 5 April Year 1, all goods bought for re-sale

	£
Sales	40,000
Less Purchases	25,000
Gross profit	15,000

Most businesses, however, will not sell all their goods in one financial year. Any stock left unsold is called **closing stock**.

When the amount of gross profit earned is being calculated it is important to include the value of the closing stock so that the figure arrived at is a true reflection of the amount of purchases bought and sold during the financial year. In the accounts of The Golf Shop, the calculations would be shown as in Figure 5.2.

Figure 5.2   The Golf Shop: Trading Account for the year Ended 5 April Year 1 closing stock

	£	£
Sales		40,000
Purchases	25,000	
Less Closing stock	*2,000*	
Cost of goods sold		*23,000*
Gross profit		*17,000*

As can be seen from Figure 5.2 by deducting the closing stock, valued at £2,000, the gross profit figure has risen from £15,000 to £17,000. In other words only £23,000 worth of stock was used during Year 1 to generate £40,000 of sales revenue.

On 6 April The Golf Shop will begin its second year of trading with the £2,000 worth of stock remaining from Year 1. Last year's closing stock thus becomes the next year's **opening** stock, and is shown as in Figure 5.3.

Figure 5.3   The Golf Shop: Trading Account for 5 April Year 2

	£	£
Sales		54,000
Opening stock	2,000	
Purchases	29,000	
	31,000	
Less Closing stock	*5,000*	
Cost of goods sold		*26,000*
Gross profit		*28,000*

In Figure 5.3, the closing stock from Year 1 has been entered as the opening stock for Year 2. The closing stock of £5,000 would then appear as opening stock at the beginning of Year 3.

Amendments included in the Trading Account

In addition to the stock adjustments made in the Trading Account there are also some other amendments which may need to be included. These relate to:

- Returns inward
- Returns outward
- Additional income – cash discounts, interest received, commission and rent received.

Returns inwards

(1) Some goods which are sold are sometimes returned by customers because they are incorrect or faulty. These must be **deducted** from the total sales figure. In the Trading Account they are shown under the heading returns inwards because they are **coming back** into the business. Once the returns have been deducted from the sales figure, the firm will know its net sales.

Returns outwards

(2) Likewise some goods which are purchased are returned to suppliers because they do not meet the specification or are incorrect in some other way. When goods are sent back to suppliers they must be **deducted** from the total purchases figure. In the Trading Account they are shown under the heading returns outwards, because they are **going out** of the business.

These amendments would appear in The Golf Shop's accounts as in Figure 5.4.

Figure 5.4   The Golf Shop: Trading Account for the year ended 5 April Year 2, returns inwards and outwards

	£	£	£
Sales			54,000
Less Returns inwards			*3,500*
Net sales			50,500

	£	£	£
Opening stock	2,000		
Add Purchases	29,000		
	31,000		
Less Returns outwards	1,500		
		29,500	
Less Closing stock		5,000	
Cost of goods sold			24,500
Gross profit			26,000

Whenever goods are delivered, someone must pay the cost of **transporting** them from the buyer to the seller. If the buyer pays it is shown in the Trading Account under "purchases" as **carriage inwards**, but if the seller pays it is shown in their Profit and Loss Account as an expense, and is called **carriage outwards**. Look at Figure 5.5.

Figure 5.5   The Golf Shop: Trading Account for the Year Ended 5 April Year 2, carriage inwards and outwards

	£	£	£
Sales			54,000
Less Returns inwards			3,500
Net sales			50,500
Opening stock	2,000		
Add Purchases	29,000		
Add Carriage inwards	1,500		
		32,500	
Less Returns Outwards		1,500	
		31,000	
Less Closing stock		5,000	
Cost of goods sold			26,000
Gross profit			24,500

Additional income

Once the gross profit has been calculated, there may be some additional income which needs to be added to this sum. When a firm receives a **cash discount** for prompt payment of an invoice, the total money saved is treated as additional income and shown under the gross profit figure as **discount received**. Other income may be in the form of **interest** received from investments, **commission** earned from sales and **rent** received from properties let.

All firms need to make a gross profit, because it is from this surplus that they will be able to pay their **expenses**, which will be shown in the Profit and Loss Account.

The Profit and Loss Account

This account as we know, summarises the firm's **trading expenses** and **deducts** them from the gross profit to calculate the **net profit**. A net profit will only be made if the gross profit exceeds total expenses. If this is not the case, a **loss** will be made because insufficient profit has been earned. The most common expenses incurred by businesses are shown in Figure 5.6, a full Trading and Profit and Loss Account for The Golf Shop.

Figure 5.6   The Golf Shop: Trading and Profit and Loss Account for the year ended 5 April Year 2

	£	£	£
Sales			54,000
Less Returns inwards			3,500
Net sales			50,500
Opening stock	2,000		
Add Purchases	29,000		
Add Carriage inwards	1,500		
		32,500	
Less Returns outwards		1,500	
		31,000	
Less Closing stock		5,000	
Cost of goods sold			26,000

	£	£	£
Gross profit			24,500
Add Discount received			1,500
			26,000
Wages	3,500		
Rent	500		
Advertising	200		
Stationery	300		
Postage	150		
Insurance	250		
Motor expenses	150		
Lighting and heating	300		
Discount allowed	60		
Carriage outwards	100		
Depreciation	340		
Bad Debts	200		
Provision for doubtful debts	100		
Total expenses			6,150
Net profit			19,850

Most of these entries do not need further explanation but five do need to be defined.

Discount allowed

When goods are sold on credit the firm must **wait for its money**. As an inducement to make customers pay on time a **cash discount** is sometimes offered. This is an expense to the firm, and is shown in the Profit and Loss Account as **discount allowed**.

Carriage outwards

Whenever goods are sold and not collected immediately by the customer, they must be **delivered**. This is a cost which must be paid either by the supplier or by the customer. If the supplier pays the cost, it is an expense to the business, and must be shown as such in the Profit and Loss Account under the heading **carriage outwards**.

Bad debts and provision for doubtful debts

Not all sales made on credit will be **settled**. During the financial year those debtors who have not paid must be classified as **bad debts**. These customers have effectively been given the goods and so this cost must be shown against profit. As a result bad debts are always recorded as an expense in the Profit and Loss Account.

In addition to bad debts the prudence concept (see Chapter 2) requires that a provision be made for those debtors who still owe money but whom it is considered likely to **default on payment**. The provision will be calculated as a percentage of total debtors, and will be shown in both the Profit and Loss Account and Balance Sheet.

In the Profit and Loss Account it will be treated as an expense so long as the amount being created, as a provision is **greater than declared the previous year**. If, however, the provision is reduced, it must be **added** to the gross profit. The reason for this is that last year profits were **understated**, because too much was provided for doubtful debts.

The amount shown as bad debts in the Profit and Loss Account will not affect the sum showed as debtors in the Balance Sheet. Any amount declared as a provision for doubtful debts, however, must be **deducted** from the debtors figure shown in the current assets section of the Balance Sheet, thereby complying with the prudence concept.

Depreciation

Whenever a business uses its fixed assets such as premises or machinery, they become progressively **worn out**. If no charge was made for using these assets the profits would be overstated. This could lead to insufficient profits being kept in the business to finance **future capital investment programmes**. "Depreciation" is the term used by accountants to provide for this wearing out of assets. It is shown first of all in the Profit and Loss Account even though it is a non-cash expense. It will also appear in the Balance Sheet to reflect the **reduction in the asset's value**. The two main methods of calculating depreciation are the straight line and the reducing balance method.

Straight Line Method

The straight line method calculates the depreciation as a **percentage of the cost of the asset**. The method takes its name from the fact that if each year's depreciation was plotted on a graph it would form a straight line, because the same amount of depreciation is charged each year. Depreciation is calculated as follows:

$$\frac{\text{Cost of asset less Residual value}}{\text{Expected useful life of asset}} = \text{Depreciation Per Annum}$$

Leisure Parks: depreciation

Leisure Parks have invested £90,000 in a new children's railway which they believe will have a life of 4 years after which its scrap value will be £5,625. We can see how the two methods differ in their way of calculating depreciation.

Straight line method

$$\frac{\text{Cost of asset less Residual value}}{\text{Expected useful life of asset}} \quad \frac{£90,000 - £5,625}{4 \text{ years}} = £21,094$$

The amount to be depreciated is therefore £21,094 per annum

Year	Cost £	Depreciation £	Net book value £
1	90,000	21,094	68,906
2	90,000	42,188	47,812
3	90,000	63,282	26,718
4	90,000	84,376	5,625

At the end of Year 4 the cost of the asset has been depreciated.

Note: to the nearest number.

Reducing balance method

Using Leisure Parks' figures of £90,000 for the investment with a scrap value of £5,625 at the end of 4 years, let us now look at the reducing balance method of calculating depreciation.

A fixed percentage is charged for depreciation each year. The basic calculation used to determine the relevant percentage is as follows:

$$r = 1 - \sqrt[n]{\frac{s}{a}} \times 100$$

n = life of asset
s = residual value
a = cost of the asset
r = rate of depreciation to be applied.

Using the Leisure Parks figures, the calculations would be :

$$1 - \sqrt[4]{\frac{£5,625}{£90,000}} = 1 - 0.5 = 0.5 \text{ or } 50\%$$

How the depreciation is calculated:
Year
1   Depreciation at 50% × £90,000 = £45,000
     £90,000 – £45,000 = Net book value £45,000

2   Depreciation at 50% × £45,000 = £22,500
     £45,000 – £22,500 = Net book value £22,500

3   Depreciation at 50% × £22,500 = £11,250
     £22,500 – £11,250 = Net book value £11,250

4   Depreciation at 50% × £11,250 = £5,625
     £11,250 – £5,625 = Net book value £5,625

Tabulating depreciation

Our information for Leisure Parks can now be presented in tabular format:

Year	Cost £	Depreciation £	Net book value £
1	90,000	45,000	45,000
2	90,000	67,500	22,500
3	90,000	78,750	11,250
4	90,000	84,375	5,625

Method of depreciation to use

Many firms adopt the straight line method because it is simple and easy to calculate. Critics of this method argue that it ignores the true rate of wear and tear. The reducing balance method addresses this problem by charging more depreciation during the **early years** of the asset's life, and there is also the advantage that the depreciation charge **declines** as repair costs **rise** with increasing use of the asset.

Trading and Profit and Loss Account concepts

Revenue expenditure

All expenditure shown in the Profit and Loss Account is collectively called "revenue expenditure" because the business derives no long-term benefit from it. Once the rent bill has been paid and the time it covers has expired, the firm has no right to stay in the premises until it makes the next payment. Such expenditure must thus be written off as an expense against profit in the Year in which it is incurred.

Matching income and expenditure

It is an accounting convention that all income earned during any financial Year will be matched against expenditure. The fact that cash has not yet been received or paid is **ignored** when the Trading and Profit and Loss Account is prepared. The sales figure will show the total invoiced value of sales, even though not all of the goods have been paid for because they have been sold on credit. Similarly the total expenses will show the amount incurred during that year, even though some invoices received have not yet been settled. This situation arises because the accounts are prepared according to what accountants call the "accruals convention" as opposed to recording receipts and payments only when money actually changes hands (see below).

Prepayments

Any money paid in advance will not relate to the **current** financial year. The sum must be deducted in the Profit and Loss Account and included in the debtors figure which will be shown in the Balance Sheet. Some people prefer to show sums paid in advance under the heading "prepayments". Whichever method is chosen, the amount prepaid must be shown as a **current asset** in the Balance Sheet, because until the next time period the money is in theory **refundable**.

Accruals

Although the firm may have incurred the expenditure the expense may not yet have been **paid**. The sum owing must be included in the current year's Profit and Loss Account and shown as a liability under current liabilities in the Balance Sheet. Once again, the sum owed can be shown by adding it to the creditors figure or showing it under the separate heading of **accruals**.

Items shown in the Balance Sheet

Whilst we have now dealt with all income and expenditure which must be shown in a Trading and Profit and Loss Account, we have not considered how such items as **premises** and **machinery** are shown in the final accounts. These items, together with the funds such as shares and loans which **finance** the business, are not shown in the Profit and Loss Account but in the Balance Sheet. This is a separate financial statement, and is explained in Chapter 6.

Study tasks

1 Identify whether the following transactions should be shown in the Trading Account or the Profit and Loss Account of the Croeso Hotel:

Transaction		Trading Account	Profit and Loss Account
(a)	Sales		
(b)	Postage		
(c)	Returns inwards		
(d)	Wages		
(e)	Depreciation		
(f)	Discount allowed		
(g)	Electricity		
(h)	Returns outwards		
(i)	Purchases		

Transaction	Trading Account	Profit and Loss Account
(j) Motor expenses		
(k) Bad debts		
(l) Closing stock		
(m) Advertising expenses		
(n) Carriage inwards		
(o) Audit fee		
(p) Carriage outwards		
(q) Interest payments		

2 Prepare a brief report for Sarah and Kate, explaining why the Croeso Hotel business may be a profitable business, but still be short of cash.

3 The Croeso Hotel has bought a rowing machine, which cost £2,500 for the Gymnasium. It is anticipated that it will have a life of five years, after which it will have a residual value of £500. Calculate the depreciation provision which must be charged against profit for each of the next 4 Years using:

> (a) the straight line
> (b) the reducing balance method

4 Sarah and Kate have just received the draft final accounts for the hotel. They can't understand why they show all of the sales and expenses, even though not all of the money has been received or paid. They feel that the accounts may be inaccurate, and have telephoned Ralph Simons, their accountant, for an explanation. How should you, as their accountant, answer their question?

5 Sarah and Kate would like to know the amount of gross profit which the Valley View bar makes for the Croeso Hotel. From the following information, prepare the bar's Trading Account for the quarter ended 31 March:

	£
Drink sales	45,590
Returns outwards	1,200
Carriage inwards	150
Purchases	18,000
Opening stock	400

Bar food sales	900
Returns inwards	50
Closing stock	5,030

6 The Croeso Hotel's Victoria Restaurant returns the following trading figures. Prepare the Restaurant's Trading Profit and Loss Account for the 6 months ended 30 June:

	£	£
Sales		62,500
Advertising	300	
Heating and lighting	2,020	
Wages	30,700	
Interest received		1,200
Purchases	22,000	
Laundry	1,800	
Carriage inwards	500	
Discount received		300
Postage	200	
Telephone	400	
Depreciation	2,700	
Closing stock	800	
Discount allowed	230	
Audit fee	2,150	
Motor expenses	150	
Cleaning materials	50	
	64,000	64,000

6 Preparing a Balance Sheet

Assets and finance of the business

The Balance Sheet is a financial statement which shows the **assets** which a firm has, together with the amount of money which is **financing** it, as at a particular date. A Balance Sheet is divided into four parts: fixed assets, capital, current assets and current liabilities. These are now explained in more detail.

Information shown in the Balance Sheet

Fixed assets

These are items of capital expenditure which are bought to assist in the **running** of the business. They are expected to have a life of more than 12 months. Examples of such **tangible** fixed assets include premises, fixtures and fittings, vehicles and equipment. It is a convention that they are shown in **order of permanence**.

As was explained in Chapter 5, most fixed assets **depreciate** through use. An amount for depreciation has to be calculated and this is entered as a non-cash expense in the Profit and Loss Account and in the Balance Sheet as an adjustment to the value of fixed assets.

In addition to the tangible fixed assets a business may have **intangible** assets. These derive their name from the fact that they **cannot be seen**, and include such items as goodwill and patent rights.

Capital

This is the amount of **long-term money** financing a business. It shows how much has been invested by the owners, and it is treated as a liability because the business **owes the owners** that sum. Any profits kept in the business increase the firm's capital and so retained profits are added to the sum shown as capital in the Balance Sheet. Similarly any losses or money taken out of the business, known as **drawings**, reduces the capital base of the firm.

Current assets

These are the **short-term assets** of a business. They are used for **trading** and will constantly be changing. They are always shown in **order of liquidity**, which measures how quickly they can be turned into cash. Stock is shown first, followed by the amount of money owed to the firm by debtors and prepayments. Finally the firm's bank and cash balances are shown.

Current liabilities

This is money **owed to suppliers or lenders**. A distinction is made between sums owed for **less** or **more than 1 year**. The former is called "current liabilities", and these include trade creditors, accruals and bank over-draft. The latter is generally referred to as long-term liabilities, because they fall due after 12 months. Bank loans and mortgages are good examples.

Presentation of the Balance Sheet

Unlike the Profit and Loss Account a firm can have its Balance Sheet drawn up in two different ways. Both are correct and it is really a matter of personal preference.

Horizontal format

The oldest method is **horizontal** and is explained first. It takes its name from the way the information is prepared horizontally across the page showing the firm's total assets and liabilities. Today Balance Sheets prepared in this way are considered old fashioned for companies but they are often used for preparing the accounts of sole traders and partners. Figure 6.1 shows the Balance Sheet entries in horizontal format and Figure 6.2 the Balance Sheet in the same format for the Tourist and Gifts and Craft Centre.

Figure 6.1   Tourist and Gifts and Craft Centre: Balance Sheet prepared in horizontal format as at the end of a financial year

Liabilities side	Assets side
Capital	Fixed Assets
Long-term money provided by the owners in the form of share capital or long-term loans from lenders of finance to the business	Long-term assets such as premises and furniture which the firm uses to earn its profits
Current Liabilities	Current Assets
Short-term money provided by lenders of funds to a business such as creditors and short-term bank loans, e.g. bank overdraft The money must be repaid within the next 12 months	Short-term assets which a firm has for trading such as stock, debtors (money owed to the firm) and cash balances
Total Liabilities =	Total Assets

Figure 6.2   The Tourist Gifts and Craft Centre: Balance Sheet as at 5 April Year 1

Capital	£	Fixed Assets	£
Capital	30,000	Premises	20,000
Add Profit	8,000	Fixtures and Fittings	13,000
	38,000		
Less Drawings	4,000		
Capital Employed	34,000		
Current Liabilities		**Current Assets**	
Creditors	6,000	Stock	2,500
		Debtors	1,000
		Bank	2,500
		Cash	1,000
	40,000		40,000

Vertical format

The second method presents the information in **vertical** format. This approach uses the same data, but prepares it in such a way that it shows the **net assets** of a business together with the capital which is **financing** them. The term "net assets" describes a firm's total assets (fixed and current) less any money owed to outside lenders and other creditors. This form of presentation makes it immediately apparent how much of the assets have been provided by the owners, thereby making a distinction between the owners and those who have lent money to the firm. Many people argue that it is easier to understand the information prepared in this way.

Although this form of presentation is comparatively recent it has grown in popularity and is now the most popular way of presenting a company Balance Sheet. Figure 6.3 shows the Balance Sheet entries in vertical format and Figure 6.4 the Balance Sheet in the same format for the Tourist Gifts and Craft Centre.

Figure 6.3   The Tourist Gifts and Craft Centre: Balance Sheet prepared in vertical format as at the end of a financial year

Fixed Assets

PLUS

Current Assets

LESS

Current Liabilities

EQUALS

Net Assets   Assets owned by the business

EQUALS

Capital   Money financing the business
                    provided by the owners

Figure 6.4   The Tourist Gifts and Craft Centre: Balance Sheet as at 5 April Year 1

Fixed Assets	£	£
Premises		20,000
Fixtures and fittings		13,000
		33,000
Current Assets		
Stock	2,500	
Debtors	1,000	
Bank	2,500	
Cash	1,000	
	7,000	
Less Current Liabilities		
Creditors	6,000	
Working capital		1,000
Net Assets		34,000
Capital		
Capital		30,000
Add Profit		8,000
		38,000
Less Drawings		4,000
Capital employed		34,000

Although the same information has been recorded by the two methods it is immediately apparent that the final figures are **different**. This is because the horizontal Balance Sheet shows a firm's **total assets and liabilities** whereas the vertical Balance Sheet shows the **net assets** of the business.

Balance Sheet concepts

Going concern

The Balance Sheet should never be taken as a **valuation** of a business because the assets are shown at their original or historical cost and not their **current market value**. The reason for this is that accountants assume that the business will continue in operation.

Depreciation

As a result the depreciation shown does not necessarily reflect the decrease in market value of the asset. Instead it is merely a way of **charging** for the **use of the asset over its working life**. If the total amount charged for depreciation is deducted from the cost price, the balance will be its net book value.

Reconciliation of money owing and owed

At the time of preparing the Balance Sheet the business is likely to **owe** money to suppliers and other creditors as well as being **owed** money.

Money **owing** is a **liability** and money **owed** is an **asset**, and both must be recorded in the Balance Sheet. Any money owing is added to the creditors figure and shown as a "current liability". Similarly any money owed is added to debtors and shown under the heading "current assets".

A provision must be made for any money owed which the firm believes will **not be paid**, and this sum must be shown in addition to any sum written off profits in the Profit and Loss Account for money lost through bad debts.

By showing the amounts owing and owed in this way the information is reconciled with all expenses and income shown in the Profit and Loss Account. The Balance Sheet therefore, shows the amount of money owing and owed at each year end.

Assets, earnings and profitability

The assets which a firm has are significant with regard to earnings and profitability. Generally the more assets, the greater the earnings and profits. It is important to understand the layout and content of a Balance Sheet, for it forms the basis of company accounts and how to interpret them. These two topics are explained in Chapters 10 and 16. Figure 6.5 shows how Youngs Breweries plc make their Balance Sheet figures accessible to those interested in the accounts.

Figure 6.5   Shows how Youngs Breweries plc make their Balance Sheet figures accessible to those interested in the accounts

Balance Sheet

WHAT WE OWN

Fixed assets £149,886,441

Current assets:
 Stocks................................£5,305,148

Debtors............................£4,521,945

Cash £424,024
 _____

TOTAL OF WHAT WE OWN...........£160,137,558

Fixed assets – What we need to run a brewery
The brewery buildings, plant, pubs, off-licence and motor vehicles.

LESS – WHAT WE OWE

Creditors £11,016,694

Bank................................£4,762,098

Loans £27,521,903
 _____

TOTAL OF WHAT WE OWE.............£43,300,695

Deferred taxation £2,977,268

Leaving what the
group is worth
(Book value)..................................£113,859,595

Creditors – For supplies of malt and hops, wines and spirits. Plus duty. VAT, tax,dividends, services and equipment.

HOW THE MONEY WAS CREATED

Shareholders £9,361,280

Revaluation
reserve £87,625,040

Past profits.................£16,873,275
 _____

£113,859,595

Shareholders – People who buy shares on the Stock Exchange and 'B' shareholders.

Current assets/stocks – What we need to trade. Malt, hops and sugar to make beer. Wine and spirits, spare parts.

Current/assets/debtors – What we are owed by tenants of the pubs, by customers and by others.

Loans – Like a mortgage on a house.

Deferred taxation – Tax to be paid in the future over many years.

Revaluation reserve – Surplus on the value of our properties.

Past profits – Money from previous years that has been ploughed back to improve the group, after the payment of dividends to shareholders.

Study tasks

1   Complete the following table:

	Fixed assets £	Current assets £	Current liabilities £	Capital £
(a)	40,000	20,000	15,000	?
(b)	?	80,000	50,000	40,000
(c)	70,000	?	25,000	90,000
(d)	50,000	25,000	?	60,000
(e)	20,000	10,000	4,000	?

2   State whether the following items of the Croeso Hotel's expenditure should be classified as **revenue** or as **capital** expenditure.

(a) Advertising the hotel in Le Monde and Le Figaro
(b) Purchasing a new microwave oven
(c) Training costs for a staff hygiene course
(d) Using hotel staff to paint the hotel bedrooms
(e) Legal fees incurred in purchasing land adjacent to the hotel
(f) Hotel cleaning bill
(g) Chef's wages.

3   Sarah and Kate have just received the hotel's latest Balance Sheet. In it are a number of terms which they have asked you to explain:

- Net assets
- Accruals
- Capital employed
- Working capital
- Shareholders' funds
- Prepayments.

4   Sarah and Kate know that the value of the fixed assets shown in the Balance Sheet does not reflect their current market value. What underlying accounting concepts govern the preparation of Balance Sheets, and why should such fixed asset figures not be used for valuation purposes?

5   Sarah and Kate run a small charity for local wildlife called Freedom which raises money for local causes. They have asked you to prepare the charity's Balance Sheet for 31 December Year 1, from the following figures:

	£
Stock	500
Cash	1,250
Creditors	150
Subscriptions in arrears	30
Building Society Account	350
Stationery	20
Subscriptions in advance	10
Debtors	40

6   From the following information calculate the net assets of each business:

	Capital liabilities	Current assets	Fixed assets	Current assets	Net assets
(a)	80,000	40,000	70,000	50,000	?
(b)	140,000	90,000	120,000	110,000	?
(c)	50,000	30,000	34,000	?	?
(d)	?	44,000	100,000	104,000	?
(e)	146,000	?	126,000	100,000	?
(f)	90,000	60,000	?	70,000	?

7 Preparing Bank Reconciliation Statements

The business and the bank

Every business needs to keep a Cash Book which will record all receipts and payments, whether they are in the form of a bank cheque or cash. This account in effect provides a record of the firm's **transactions with its bank**. The bank will also keep records of the cheques and money the business pays into its account, together with receipts and payments from debtors and creditors who make use of banking payment facilities such as standing orders and direct debits.

From time to time the business will receive a **Bank Statement**. This will show all of the financial transactions for a set accounting period. Most businesses will receive a monthly statement, but very large companies may find this too infrequent and may need daily statements because of the large number of transactions which they have. In theory the balance on the firm's Cash Account should be the same as the amount shown on the Bank Statement, but in practice this is rarely the case.

Why may the balance in the Cash Book and the amount in the Bank Statement not agree?

The two accounting statements may fail to show the same balances for **three** main reasons.

Financial transactions recorded incorrectly

There may be errors in either the Cash Book or the Bank Statement if either **party has failed** to record the financial transaction correctly. Although most errors will be made by the firm it is not unheard of for the bank to make a mistake. For instance the bank may debit or credit the wrong bank account, and then such an error will be brought to its attention by the customer who has identified the problem.

Transactions affecting the Bank Account not entered in the Cash Book

Some entries on the Bank Statement may not yet have been written up in the Cash Book because the firm has **no knowledge of them**. The bank may have debited the account with a service or interest charge, for example, and this amount will not be apparent until the firm receives its Bank Statement. These transactions must then be recorded in the Cash Book.

Transactions accounted for because of timing differences

One of the reasons for the difference is the **time taken** for transactions to appear both in the Cash Book and on the Bank Statement. A cheque may have been sent to a supplier. This will then have been entered in the Cash Book but will not appear on the Bank Statement until it is presented for payment. Similarly the firm may have received a cheque and debited the Cash Book but because it was paid into the bank just before closing time it has not yet been credited to its account.

These differences make it necessary for a **Reconciliation Statement** to be prepared by the firm so that the balance in the Cash Book can be reconciled with that shown in the Bank Statement.

Bank Reconciliation Statement

This accounting statement will **identify any errors** made by the firm or its bankers. Any error found must be **corrected**. Once this has been done the next step is to credit the Cash Book with any unknown payments such as bank charges and debit the account in the Nominal Ledger for such expenses. Finally any errors between the Cash Book and the Bank Statement brought about by timing differences must be listed. Looking at the Nutmeg Vegetarian Restaurant's problems will help to clarify this process.

The Nutmeg Vegetarian Restaurant: Cash Book/ Bank Statement differences

On 5 May Year 1 the Nutmeg Vegetarian Restaurant's Cash Book showed a balance of £510. On the same day the manager Jonathan Harrington received a Bank Statement which showed a balance of £615. Jonathan has looked at the two statements and has found **five** key differences:

(1) The bank has paid £15 to cover the restaurant's subscription to a business journal. No entry has yet been made in the restaurant's Cash Book.

(2) The restaurant has received a cheque from a corporate customer for £300 which has been entered in the Cash Book but has not yet been credited to their Bank Account.

(3) On 3 May the bank debited £30 from the restaurant's bank account to cover bank charges. No record of this payment has yet been made in the restaurant's Cash Book.

(4) The following cheques written to pay suppliers and recorded in the restaurant's Cash Book on 3 May have not yet been presented to the bank for payment:

	£
Wheatsheaf Bakers	100
R. and L. Grocers	40
Wilson's Garage	250

(5) The bank has credited to the restaurant's account a £60 claim from its insurance company. No entry has yet been made in the Cash Book.

Correcting the Cash Book

The first task is to correct the restaurant's Cash Book by entering any transaction which has already been recorded in the Bank Statement but which has not yet been entered in the Cash Book, as in Figure 7.1.

Figure 7.1   Correcting the Cash Book: entries made

Dr		CASH BOOK		Cr
		£		£
May 5	Balance	510	Subscription	15
	Insurance claim	60	Bank Charges	30
			Balance	525
		___		___
		570		570

The Cash Book is now correct. The two payments which have been made by the bank have been credited to the Cash Book while the receipt of cash (insurance claim) has been debited to the Account. A bank reconciliation can now be prepared, as in Figure 7.2.

Figure 7.2   Bank Reconciliation: entries made

BANK RECONCILIATION 5 MAY		
		£
Balance as per Bank Statement		615
Add cheque not yet credited		300
		915
Less cheques drawn but not yet presented		
	£	
Wheatsheaf Bakers	100	
R. and L. Grocers	40	
Wilson's Garage	250	
		390
Adjusted bank balance		525

By adding the cheque which has not yet been credited to the figure shown on the Bank Statement the firm will know the total amount of money it has at the bank. By deducting the sum of the cheques for payment which have not yet been paid by the bank the firm will reconcile the Bank Account balance with that of its Cash Book.

Need to control cash and payments

Management need to know their true day-to-day cash position so that they are in control of their receipts and payments. The real value of this concept is explained in Chapter 17, on working capital management.

Study tasks

1 Why do Sarah and Kate need to prepare a Bank Reconciliation Statement when they already keep a Cash Book and also receive a Bank Statement?

2 Give **four** examples of entries which will appear on the Croeso Hotel's Bank Statement before they have been entered in the Cash Book.

3 Give **two** examples of entries which would appear in the Croeso Hotel's Cash Book but not on its Bank Statement.

4 The Cash Book on 1 February shows that the Croeso Hotel has a balance of £2,790.60 Dr. The Bank Statement shows a different balance. On investigation Sarah and Kate have found that a cheque for £78.50 has not yet been credited to the account and that a transfer for £131.60 to the hotel's current account has not yet been made. From this information, prepare a Bank Reconciliation Statement.

5 The Cash Book of the Croeso Hotel showed a Dr. balance of £1849.20 on 1 May. The Bank Statement for the same date showed a different balance. On investigation the following information was discovered:

> **(a)** Two cheques for £1,310.96 and £318.80, although entered in the Cash Book have not yet appeared on the Bank Statement
>
> **(b)** Bank charges £18.80 have not been entered in the Cash Book
>
> **(c)** A debtor has paid £200 direct into the firm's Bank Account
>
> **(d)** A cheque for £1,894 has not yet been credited to the Account
>
> **(e)** Interest owed on bank account £800 has been deducted from the firm's Account
>
> **(f)** A cheque received from a debtor £510 has been returned by the bank marked "Refer to Drawer". No entry has yet been made in the Cash Book.

Reconcile the Bank Statement with the Cash Book.

6 The Cash Book for the Croeso Hotel's Gymnasium showed a Dr balance of £469 on 30 June. The Bank Statement showed a different balance and Kate has found the following differences:

> **(a)** A cheque for £157 paid into the account on 30 June is not shown on the Statement
>
> **(b)** Two cheques issued to suppliers for £163.20 and £100 have not yet been presented to the bank for payment
>
> **(c)** The bank has charged a handling fee of £3.40
>
> **(d)** £100 has been paid by standing order to the General Leasing Company
>
> **(e)** Sarah paid a cheque for £90.20 into the Account, but forgot to enter it into the Cash Book.

Reconcile the Bank Statement with the Cash Book.

8 Accounting for Wages

Weekly wages and monthly wages

Wages are usually paid to weekly-paid staff and are generally calculated on the number of hours worked. A swimming pool attendant might work a 40 hour week and be paid £4 an hour, making the weekly wage £160. A Leisure Centre Manager is more likely to be paid a fixed salary for a year, and to receive it in monthly instalments regardless of the hours worked.

Gross and net pay

The gross pay is the amount of money which the employee earns **before deductions**. Take-home pay is less because the employer must deduct any money due for income tax and National Insurance. The employer then pays this direct to the Inland Revenue.

Income tax, National Insurance contributions and other deductions

Income tax

The government needs money to pay for schools, hospitals, defence and other public services such as roads. These items can only be paid for by raising taxes. One large source of government revenue is received by taxing workers on the income which they earn. Income tax is said to be a **progressive** tax, which means that the more a person earns, the greater amount of tax they have to pay. All people who are employed have their tax payments deducted from their wages by their employer, who then ensures that the money is paid to the Inland Revenue. In effect the employer has become an unpaid tax collecting agent for the Inland Revenue. The system is generally referred to as "Pay As You Earn", which is usually abbreviated to PAYE.

People running their own business and those working on a self-employed basis may be outside the PAYE system and responsible for their own tax affairs with the Inland Revenue.

National Insurance

Employers and employees have to pay National Insurance contributions (NICs) to cover the benefits available from the National Health Service. These contributions, like income tax, are payable in rising amounts on the sum earned. All employees earning above the minimum threshold for tax and National Insurance contributions must have the necessary amount deducted from their wages. The Inland Revenue produce tables showing the amount payable so as to make the calculations easier for employers.

Other deductions

Some large firms are willing to make further deductions if the employee agrees. For example, deductions could be made for payments to be made into a pension scheme, to a trade union or into a holiday savings scheme. There is, however, no legal duty for an employer to provide these services although most large organisations are happy to do so.

Accounting for wages and salaries

The amounts paid in wages and salaries must be recorded using the same double entry method as described in Chapters 3 and 4.

Control Accounts

The firm will need to set up three new **Control Accounts**:

(**1**) Wages Control Account
(**2**) PAYE Control Account
(**3**) National Insurance Control Account.

Ledger entries

Once this has been done the person responsible for the payroll must calculate the total wages and salary paid by the business inclusive of employer's National Insurance contributions. The following entries will then be made in the ledgers:

Double Entry Flow Chart

	Gross pay	Tax	NIC Employer's	Net Pay	NIC Employees'	
P/L A/C Wages and Salaries	Dr				Dr	1 Journal
Wages Control A/C				Cr		
PAYE Control A/C		Cr				
NIC Control A/C			Cr		Cr	
Credit Bank		Dr	Dr	Dr	Dr	2 Journal

Each week or month the total of employees' tax and National Insurance contributions must be debited to the Gross Wages Control Account with the respective amounts due being credited to the PAYE Control Account and National Insurance Control Account. The credit balances in the Wages, PAYE and National Insurance Contributions Control Accounts will be removed by debiting the accounts once payments to the employees and Inland Revenue are made. Any other deductions from the employee's salary should not be debited to the Wages Control Account and credited to the respective liability account until the amount is paid, when the account will be debited with the sum paid. Rebecca Davis's wages payments at the City Gym will help to make this clear.

The City Gym: wages transactions

Rebecca Davis, who manages the City Gym, is about to pay her staff wages. It is company policy to pay all employees monthly, and all wages are paid direct into employee Bank Accounts.

On 1 September Year 2 the Ledger Accounts of the City Gym had the following credit balances:

	£
PAYE Control Account	6,500
NIC Control Account	1,800

The gym's wage records for October Year 2 contained the following information:

	£
Total gross pay	13,790
PAYE Control	3,700
Employer's NIC	1,600
Employees' NIC	900
Net Amounts paid to employees	8,510

During October the gym paid £2,400 to the Inland Revenue, being made up of £1,580 income tax and £820 National Insurance contributions.

The City Gym: Ledger Accounts

These transactions are now illustrated in the City Gym's Ledger Accounts, in Figure 8.1.

Figure 8.1   The City Gym: Ledger Accounts

Dr	WAGES CONTROL ACCOUNT		Cr
	£		£
Bank net pay	8,510	Profit and Loss	8,510
	8,510		8,510

	PAYE CONTROL ACCOUNT		
	£		£
Bank (tax paid)	1,580	Balance	6,500
		Profit and Loss	3,700
Balance	8,620		
	10,200		10,200

	NIC CONTROL ACCOUNT		
	£		£
Bank NIC paid	820	Balance	1,800
Balance	3,480	Employees' Profit and Loss	900
		Employer's Profit and loss	1,600
	4,300		4,300

Costs of employing staff

Apart from complying with the legal requirements of paying wages managers need to know the full costs of employing staff. Unless this is known it will be impossible to calculate the firm's **costs**, a topic which is discussed in more detail in Chapter 13.

Study tasks

At first, Sarah and Kate thought that they would not need to employ any full-time staff. The business, however, has been so successful that three full-time jobs have been created. Catherine Jenkins has been recruited to manage all reservations and reception work; Hugh Roberts has joined the hotel as Head Chef and Elaine Bates is to be in charge of the grounds, developing sports facilities. The weekly wage bill is shown below:

- **Catherine Jenkins** is married. She currently earns £200 a week.
- **Hugh Roberts** is single. He has a £40,000 mortgage and pays £15 a month into a private pension plan. Hugh earns £200 a week.
- **Elaine Bates** is married. She and her husband have a £50,000 mortgage which is in his name. Elaine pays £20 a month private medical insurance for her mother who is 66.

---

1 Which forms must be completed by Sarah and Kate for the Croeso Hotel staff who are on PAYE.?

2 What personal allowances are each of the new three full-time staff entitled to?

3 Apart from the three full-time employees the hotel also has four part-time staff. Their names and wages are shown below:

	£ a week
• Trevor Lewis	£60
• Daphne Trowbridge	£50
• William Drummond	£30
• Monica Petrocelli	£42

Using the current tax and National Insurance tables calculate the amount of income tax and National Insurance owed to the Inland Revenue for these employees.

4   Prepare wage slips for the four part-time employees, showing the amount they have been paid together with all deductions. Assume an income tax rate of 25p in the £.

5   Prepare the Wages Accounts as they should be recorded in the Croeso Hotels' Ledgers using the double entry system.

6   Daphne Trowbridge has just told Sarah that she wishes to leave at the end of the month. What documents must be completed for Daphne to take to her new employer?

9 Recording Value Added Tax

Paying VAT

Value Added Tax (VAT) is an indirect tax which is collected by Customs and Excise. It is charged on most goods and services bought by consumers. The rate of VAT is set by the government, usually in the Budget.

All business people are liable to pay the tax, but those that become VAT **registered** are allowed in most cases to offset tax paid from that received. The two main exemptions are entertainment expenses and the purchase of motor cars. All other tax payments will be recoverable provided the business has registered for VAT.

The level of **turnover** which a business has determines whether or not it should register for VAT. Currently the government requires firms with a turnover above a set level to register with the Customs and Excise. This means that all the products or services sold by the business (its **outputs**) will be subject to the tax unless they are exempt. If a holiday camp sells bread in its shop it will not be subject to VAT; guests will, however, have to pay the tax on all other goods and services such as meals, accommodation, and laundry.

Those firms with a turnover of less than the set level will still have to pay VAT on their purchases (**inputs**) but they do not have to charge VAT on the goods and services (**outputs**) which they sell unless they register voluntarily.

The principles of VAT

Before setting up accounting records it is important to understand the taxation principles involved. This is best illustrated by a travel agency's transactions.

Imresh Patel's travel agency

Imresh Patel intends to purchase some new furniture for his travel agency from a local office supplier. He has decided to purchase five new

84

desks which have cost £1,116.25 including VAT The supplier had purchased the desks from a local manufacturer and so three different parties have been involved in this financial transaction. This can be seen in Figure 9.1.

Figure 9.1   Imresh Patel: collection and payment of VAT: entries made

Stages in the collection and payment of VAT

Manufacturer	Retailer		Customer
	Price before 17.5% VAT	VAT	Selling price
	£	£	£
Purchases materials and makes desks	300	52.50	352.50
Sells desks to retailer	650	113.75	763.75
VAT payable to Customs		61.25	

VAT payable by the manufacturer is **deducted** from that received from the retailer; in this way each party only pays the **difference** between VAT paid and that received

Retailer

	£	£	£
Buys desks from manufacturer	650	113.75	763.75
Sells desks to customer	950	166.25	1,116.25
VAT payable to Customs		52.50	

Offset of VAT against tax collected

Imresh Patel has just paid £166.25 VAT, but he will be able to offset this sum against any tax which he has collected from customers. If he had collected £400 from the sale of holidays to customers he would owe the Customs and Excise the difference between what he had received and what he had paid. The amount payable to Customs and Excise would be:

	£
Tax collected from customers	400.00
Less tax payable	166.25
Balance due to Customs and Excise	233.75

Recording VAT

It is important to remember that a business does not make any profit out of VAT which it charges customers. As a result all sales and purchases, be they on credit or for cash, should be recorded excluding VAT.

River Valley Holiday Park

Ledger accounting for VAT

River Valley Holiday Park receives £3,525 from guests staying at its lodges. The Park charges include VAT at 17.5% and so its total receipts are made up of sales of £3,000 and VAT of £525. The tax collected will not be shown in the Profit and Loss Account and so the necessary ledger accounting entries to record the sales will be:

			£
(Date)	**Debit**	Cash or Debtors	3,525
(Date)	**Credit**	Sales	3,000
(Date)	**Credit**	VAT Account	525

If the Park has bought confectionery for its campers' shop for £1,175 then the amount paid for VAT must be deducted from the purchases, provided that the business can recover the tax. The tax collected will not be shown in the Profit and Loss Account and so the necessary accounting entries to record the purchases will be:

			£
(Date)	**Debit**	Purchases	1,000
(Date)	**Debit**	VAT Account	175
(Date)	**Credit**	Trade Creditors	1,175

If the VAT cannot be reclaimed it simply increases the cost of the goods or services purchased.

Recording VAT in the Day Books

Credit sales and purchases

All credit sales will be recorded in the Sales Day Book and any credit purchases will be shown in the Purchases Day Book. It is a good idea to separate the VAT payment from either the purchase or sale. This is best carried out as in Figure 9.2.

Figure 9.2   Sales and Purchases Day Book and VAT: entries made

Sales Day Book
Using the figures for River Valley Holiday Park:

Date	Sales	VAT	Total
	£	£	£
	3,000	525	3,525

Purchases Day Book
Using the figures for River Valley Holiday Park:

Date	Purchases	VAT	Total
	£	£	£
	1,000	175	1,175

Credit and cash sales

It is important to distinguish between credit and cash sales when recording VAT. Whenever a credit sale or purchase is made there is no need to show a separate entry for the VAT in the Cash Book. This is because the tax input or output is incurred when the **sale is made**, and not when the cash is received or paid. This is not so when recording cash purchases or sales, however. In such instances, a **separate column** showing the VAT must be kept because the tax has been incurred once

the financial transaction has been made. As a result the VAT received
(**input**) from the sale must be credited to the VAT Account and the VAT
payable (output) must be debited. The Cash Book will now look like
Figure 9.3.

Figure 9.3   Debit and Credit Side of a Cash Book and VAT

Debit side					
Date	**Narrative (Details)**	**Sales Ledger £**	**Cash Sales £**	**VAT Account £**	**Total £**
Credit side					
Date	**Narrative (Details)**	**Purchases Ledger**	**Cash Purchases**	**VAT**	**Total**

Petros Haji's Kebab House

Petros Haji has just finished his second year's trading at the Kebab
House. The accounts inclusive of VAT show all entries up to and
including 31 December Year 2 (see Figure 9.4).

Figure 9.4   Petros Haji's Kebab House Accounts inclusive of VAT

Debtors and Sales	**£**
Sales Ledger Control a/c 31 Dec Year 1	7,500
Sales	47,000
Discount allowed	1,000
Cash received	30,000

Creditors and Purchases	**£**
Purchases Ledger Control a/c 31 Dec Year 1	4,500
Purchases	25,000
Discount received	400
Cash paid	15,000

Recording VAT payments

At 31 December the Kebab House owed £800 to Customs and Excise. During the first quarter payments to Customs and Excise amounted to £1,500. Assuming a VAT rate of 17.5%, how should Petros record this information? He will need three Accounts:

(a) Debtors' Control Account
(b) Creditors' Control Account
(c) VAT Control Account.

Figure 9.5 shows the entries in each of these.

Figure 9.5 Petros Haji's Kabab House: VAT entries in the Accounts

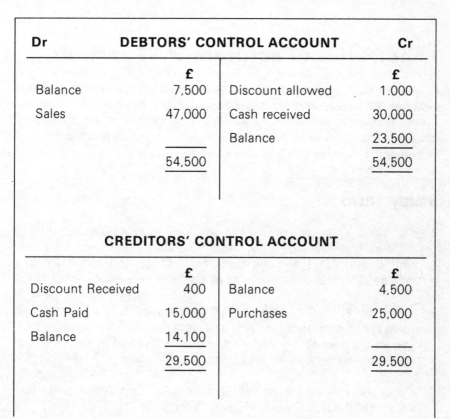

Dr	DEBTORS' CONTROL ACCOUNT		Cr
	£		£
Balance	7,500	Discount allowed	1.000
Sales	47,000	Cash received	30,000
		Balance	23,500
	54,500		54,500

CREDITORS' CONTROL ACCOUNT			
	£		£
Discount Received	400	Balance	4,500
Cash Paid	15,000	Purchases	25,000
Balance	14,100		
	29,500		29,500

Dr		VAT CONTROL ACCOUNT		Cr
	£			**£**
		Balance		800.00
Purchases 17.5%/117.5 × £25,000		Sales 17,5%/117.5 × 47,000		
	3,723.40			7,000.00
Cash paid	1,500.00			
Balance	2,576.60			
	7,800.00			7,800.00

Importance of accurate VAT records

Customs and Excise are just one of the many outside parties who require accurate financial information relating to the business. By keeping accurate records the costs of a VAT inspection can be minimised because all the necessary information will be immediately available.

Study tasks

1 Sarah and Kate have decided to purchase three single, two double and four bunk beds for the Croeso Hotel. The single beds are £125, the doubles £240 and the bunk beds £150. The retailers prices include VAT. Calculate the price of the beds before VAT at 17.5%.

2 Gwen Jones the Croeso Hotel gift shop assistant has just received some Welsh cardigans from the local wool mill. The prices before VAT are Lamb's wool £35, Aran £25 and Lamb's wool and Cashmere £65. Calculate the price of each garment including VAT at 17.5%.

3 Roger runs his own business as an interior decorator. He has just come into the hotel bar where Kate is working:

Kate	Hello, Roger How are you?
Roger	Terrible. The van's been broken and I've just got it back from the garage. Do you know just the VAT on the bill was £150 so you can imagine the total bill. Its never fair that this tax should fall on us business people.
Kate	Are you registered for VAT?
Roger	Well I've only just started my business . . .

Explain to Roger the principles of VAT, and whether or not he does owe Customs and Excise the £150.

4 The Croeso Hotel has collected £2,500 in VAT from customers. The hotel has incurred £900 VAT:

(**a**) Calculate how much money is owed to Customs and Excise

(**b**) State in which Day Books the VAT details sould be recorded.

5 Last month the Croeso Hotel had sales of £16,100 and Purchases of £9,200. Assuming a VAT rate of 15%, show the appropriate entries in the Sales Day Book and Purchases Day Book.

6 Sarah and Kate have just finished their second year's trading. The accounts inclusive of VAT show all entries up to and including 31 March Year 2:

Debtors and Sales	£
Sales Ledger Control a/c 31 March Year 1	12,000
Sales	37,000
Discount allowed	1,300
Cash received	27,000

Creditors and Purchases	£
Purchases Ledger Control a/c 31 March Year 1	3,750
Purchases	18,000
Discount received	370
Cash paid	14,300

At the 31 March the Croeso Hotel owed £650 to suppliers. During the first quarter payments to Customs and Excise amounted to £1,400. Assuming a VAT rate of 17.5%, how should the Croeso Hotel record this information? Show:

(a) Debtors' Control Account
(b) Creditors' Control Account
(c) VAT Control Account.

10 Preparing Company Accounts

Why keep accounts?

In law there is no legal duty for a sole trader to keep accounts in a set format, although it obviously makes sense for them to do so because they have to deal with the tax authorities. Accounts are also necessary from the management angle in order to review how well the business is performing. Companies, however, **must by law** keep accounts and comply with the legislation which is mainly contained in the Companies Acts.

The company and the law

Before explaining company accounts it is necessary to have a working knowledge of the main requirements of company law.

Legal entity

A company, unlike a sole trader's business, is a **legal entity**. In the case of the sole trader it is only the owner who can make contracts and enter into business relations. Companies are not in this situation as they have their own legal identity. They can therefore, **make contracts**, **employ people**, and **purchase** other businesses in their own name.

Limited liability

In addition they can have the right to limited liability which has been confirmed on them by Acts of Parliament. This means that, unlike a sole trader, the maximum loss which an owner can suffer is the extent of their **shareholdings**. Whilst not all companies choose limited liability the majority do. This privilege is not without obligations, the main one being that copies of Annual Accounts must be filed with the **Registrar of Companies** at Companies House. This is why some companies prefer not to have limited liability status.

Separation of ownership

Companies also have the added advantage of allowing the management function to be separated from the ownership of the business. Shareholders can invest in a company by purchasing shares without having to be concerned with its day-to-day operation and control.

The legal process of forming a company

Whereas there are no legal requirements to be satisfied before a sole trader may begin trading a company must follow certain procedures.

It takes **two people** to form a company. One must be the director and the other the **secretary**: one person may not hold the same post. Many people seek the advice of a solictor before forming a company whilst others approach specialist firms to carry out this task for them. There is no legal requirement to do this, but it is advisable to gain professional help before starting a company.

Registration: private and public companies

All companies must be **registered** with Companies House. There are **two** types of company. **Private** companies have a share capital of **less than £50,000; public** companies (plcs) have a share capital of **£50,000 or more**. The large companies which have become High Street names such as Forte, Bass Charington and Ladbrokes are good examples. Although plcs are more well known the majority of companies are private.

Registration forms: Certificate of Incorporation and Certificate of Trading

There are a number of forms which must be completed before a company can be formed. There are a number of regulations relating to the name of the company. Certain words, such as "Association", "Assurance" and "Royal", require the **consent** of the Secretary of State for Trade and Industry before they can be used in the title. Once registered, a **Certificate of Incorporation** will be issued but if the company is public it must also receive a **Certificate of Trading** before it can commence business.

Memorandum and Articles

Along with the application form two further documents must be submitted. These are the **Memorandum of Association** and the **Articles of Association**. Both of these legal documents govern the company's dealings with outside parties and its own internal rules and regulations:

- **Memorandum of Association**

A company's dealings with its **external environment** is governed by its Memorandum of Association. The information included in this document is the company name, the address of its registered office, the objectives of the company, the amount of share capital and a statement confirming that it has limited liability and the maximum limit of the company's borrowing powers.

- **Articles of Association**

This second document covers the **internal organisation** of the company. The rights of different types of shareholders, and how the shares can be issued and transferred, the reasons and dates for holding company meetings together with the powers of the directors, must all be explained.

Both of these documents must be kept at the registered Head Office and must be available for **inspection** during reasonable hours by any **shareholder**. The Certificate of Incorporation should be similarly displayed at the Head Office.

Statutory books

A company must also keep what are generally referred to as the "statutory books". Every company with limited liability must keep registers of:

- Members
- Directors' shareholdings
- Directors and secretaries
- Mortgages and charges.

Minute book

In addition to these registers, the company must keep a minute book for recording the minutes of **general and directors' meetings**.

The structure of company Final Accounts

Companies only have to show **certain information** in their published accounts. The reason for this is that if they had to disclose all of their costs, for example, it could handicap their competitive position. Much of the information will be disclosed in **notes to the accounts**, and these must be read if one is to fully understand the figures. We have used Cadbury's Accounts to illustrate the format of company accounts and the items which appear in them.

Look further at Cadbury's Profit and Loss Account in Figure 10.1.

Figure 10.1   Cadbury Schweppes plc: Profit and Loss Account

GROUP PROFIT AND LOSS ACCOUNT	Year 2 £m	Year 1 £m
Turnover	3,232.3	3,146.1
Cost of sales	(1,735.9)	(1,738.4)
Gross Profit	1,496.4	1,407.7
Distribution costs, including marketing	(831.3)	(798.1)
Administration expenses	(299.0)	(276.6)
Other operating income/(charges)	(3.6)	0.9
Trading Profit	362.5	333.9
Share of profits of associated undertakings	10.9	2.9
Net interest	(57.0)	(57.0)
Profit on Ordinary Activities Before Taxation	316.4	279.6
Tax on profit on ordinary activities	(88.0)	(78.0)
Profit on Ordinary Activities After Taxation	228.4	201.6
Profit attributable to minority interests	(25.2)	(22.2)
Preference dividends	(9.0)	(3.4)

continued

	Year 2 £m	Year 1 £m
Profit Attributable to Ordinary Shareholders	194.2	176.0
Dividends to ordinary shareholders	(88.0)	(80.2)
Profit Retained For The Year	106.2	95.8
Retained by:		
Cadbury Schweppes plc	74.3	53.2
Subsidiary undertakings	27.9	41.2
Associated undertakings	4.0	1.4
	106.2	95.8
Earnings Per Ordinary Share of 25p	27.73p	25.29p

Source: Cadbury Schweppes plc.

Information which must be disclosed

The Companies Acts require certain information to be disclosed about the company's income, expenses and uses or appropriation of profits. They are free to disclose any other information if they believe it will benefit the business to do so.

Income

The company must provide information about its turnover, income from investments, rental income and any profits or losses arising from the sale of fixed assets.

Expenses

Not all expenses have to be disclosed but the following **must be shown**: staff costs, directors' emoluments (salary), employees' emoluments, interest payments, hire of plant, auditing fees, depreciation and any reduction in the value of investments.

Uses or appropriation of profit

The Profit and Loss Account must show the amount of money paid in tax, any profit used to write off goodwill, and transfers to the reserves and finally the amount of money paid as dividends to the shareholders.

Profit and Loss Account terminology

Many of the terms in the Cadbury's accounts will already be familiar to you. An explanation is given here of some terms that may be new to you.

Turnover

This is the technical term for **sales**. The company must show the geographical location where goods have been sold, unless the directors believe that it would be harmful to do so. The sales figure will be **net of VAT**.

Trading profit

This is the profit which has been **earned from trading**. It excludes interest payments, as these are seen as financing costs and not operating ones. The trading profit is most akin to the sole trader's net profit.

Net interest

Most companies will borrow and lend money. The net interest figure is calculated by subtracting interest paid from that received. If the figure is shown in brackets it means that the company has **paid out** more interest than it has **earned**.

Profit on ordinary activities before taxation

This is the profit which the company has earned **before** taking into account profits which may have been made from selling fixed assets or other businesses.

Profit on ordinary activities after taxation

Companies have to pay **Corporation Tax** on their profits. The profits which are left after tax can be used for paying dividends and for re-investing in the business.

Profits attributable to ordinary shareholders

Once the tax has been paid, some of the profits will be shared by the preference shareholders and any minority interests. The preference shareholders are entitled to a **fixed rate of dividend** as long as there are sufficient profits.

Profits from subsidiaries

Many large companies own other companies. These are called **subsidiaries**. If all of the shares have been bought then they are wholly owned subsidiaries but sometimes only a percentage will have been acquired. In such cases not all of the profits will belong to the company. The shares not owned are referred to as the "minority interests", and so a deduction in profits has to be made for the profits from subsidiaries which are owed to these minority interests.

Dividends

Shareholders are entitled to receive dividends: these are a share of the company's profits. The company will set aside a sum of money which, once divided amongst the number of shares, will determine the dividend which **each shareholder will receive**.

Profit retained for the year

These are the profits which belong to the ordinary shareholders but which are **kept back** in the company to **finance future investments**. They are reserves, and will be shown in the Balance Sheet. If in the future profits fall but the directors wish to maintain the same dividend, (see also Chapter 18) then these profits may be used.

Earnings per share

This calculation shows what each £ invested in the business as share capital can **earn**. Shareholders are interested in the return which can be earned from their investment, and so they like to see an increase in the earnings per share figure.

Now look at Cadbury's Balance Sheet, in Figure 10.2.

Figure 10.2   Cadbury Schweppes plc: Balance Sheet

BALANCE SHEETS

	GROUP		COMPANY	
	Year 2	Year 1	Year 2	Year 1
	£m	£m	£m	£m
Fixed Assets				
Intangible assets	308.0	304.0	–	–
Tangible assets	1,054.2	978.8	13.2	16.8
Investments	34.2	16.7	943.0	938.9
	1,396.4	1,299.5	956.2	955.7
Current Assets				
Stocks	331.8	328.2	–	–
Debtors	578.9	554.1	278.3	113.4
Investments	262.4	118.0	5.0	5.1
Cash at bank and in hand	85.0	62.6	–	–
	1,258.1	1,062.9	283.3	118.5
Current Liabilities				
Creditors: amounts falling due within one year				
Borrowings	(138.2)	(136.3)	(225.0)	(175.0)
Other	(894.8)	(825.9)	(131.9)	(98.4)
Net Current Assets (Liabilities)	225.1	100.7	(73.6)	(154.9)
Total Assets Less Current Liabilities	1,621.5	1.400.2	882.6	800.8
Non-current Liabilities				
Creditors: amounts falling due after more than one year				
Borrowings	(542.0)	(407.9)	(53.9)	(54.2)
Other	(37.0)	(12.0)	(21.6)	(26.4)
Provisions for liabilities and charges	(53.5)	(96.4)	0.4	0.5
	(632.5)	(516.3)	(75.1)	(80.1)
	989.0	883.9	807.5	720.7
Capital and Reserves				
Called up share capital	175.9	174.7	175.9	174.7
Share premium account	393.8	381.6	393.8	381.6
Revaluation reserve	99.9	95.8	1.7	2.4
Profit and loss account	207.1	115.8	236.1	162.0
	876.7	767.9	807.5	720.7
Minority interests	112.3	116.0	–	–
	989.0	883.9	807.5	720.7

Source: Cadbury Schweppes plc.

Cadbury's Balance Sheet follows the same layout as described in Chapter 6 but contains more information.

Balance Sheet terminology

In order to understand a company Balance Sheet, you will need to understand the following terms.

- Fixed assets

These are the **long-term** assets of the business which are used to trade. Most plcs will have under this heading intangible, tangible and long-term investments:

- Intangible assets

These are always shown first, and relate to assets which have been acquired to provide a **long-term benefit** for the company. Examples will be goodwill and development costs, patents and trade marks.

- Tangible assets

These represent the normal **fixed assets** which everyone expects a business to have, such as land and buildings, fixtures and fittings and plant and machinery. Tangible assets are always shown in **order of permanence**, and the cost price or revaluation of the assets must be shown, together with the cumulative depreciation and the assets' net book value.

- Long-term investments

Many companies will purchase shares or government loan stock if they believe that a greater return can in the relative short term be gained by investing in **financial securities** instead of tangible fixed assets. If the company directors intend to hold these securities for **more than 1 year**, then they must be shown as fixed assets.

Current assets

These are a company's **short-term assets** and are used to trade. They are always shown in **order of liquidity**, with the **most illiquid** being shown first. It is important here to look at the Notes to the Accounts, which will provide more detail about the composition of the current assets and give a greater insight into a company's current assets.

Liabilities

Any money **provided by creditors** must be shown as a liability. Liabilities can be put into two categories.

- Those liabilities which must be paid **within 12 months** of the Balance Sheet date such as trade creditors, taxation payments and short-term loans.

- Creditors who must be paid **after 12 months** are shown under a separate heading and mainly consist of providers of long-term debt funds to the company (see Chapter 19).

Loan Stock: debt securities, debentures and convertibles

Companies can raise long-term finance by selling what are called **debt securities** to investors. These entitle the investor to a fixed or variable rate of interest for a specified time period. The loan may be **secured** or **unsecured**. If it is secured then the lenders will have the right to liquidate company assets in the event of non-payment of interest or capital. The main types of loan stock are referred to as debentures, and secured and unsecured loan stock.

There is one last type of loan stock; this is a hybrid and is known as **convertible loan stock**. This entitles the holder to exchange loan stock for shares. The change can take place at certain times and it is a good way of allowing a company to replace its debt capital with share capital. Convertible loan stock is often offered to existing shareholders at a favourable price as a reward for already having invested in the company. It is also a useful way of enabling a company to reduce its amount of borrowed capital thereby lowering its level of **gearing** (we shall explain the concept of gearing in Chapter 19).

Capital and reserves

This shows the amount of money which has been provided by the owners to finance the company. It will show the **amount** and **composition** of the share capital, together with the **reserves** which are financing the business:

- Authorised, called up and unissued capital

When a company is registered the directors must state in the Memorandum of Association the company's **authorised capital**. Whilst the whole amount does not have to be issued to shareholders, the company must pay stamp duty on the registered amount of capital.

The words "called up capital" means that shares have been **issued** to shareholders and that they have been **fully paid for**.

Unissued capital is the difference between a company's authorised capital and its issued capital, and the directors may chose to issue it in the future should the business need additional funds.

- Preference shares

These are shares which carry a **fixed rate of dividend**. As a result they are more akin to loan stock and from a financial analysis point of view are generally treated as such. Nevertheless the preference shareholders are owners of the business who are entitled to a fixed rate of dividend, provided that the company is profitable, **before** any ordinary shareholders receive a dividend. Sometimes the Articles of Association will state that they are entitled to receive a share of the assets upon liquidation before ordinary shareholders.

- Ordinary shares

The ordinary share capital represents the amount of money provided by the **ordinary shareholders** which is financing the business. The shares will be for a certain sum of money (such as a £1 Ordinary Share) and this will be referred to as its **nominal value**. The ordinary shareholders, together with the preference shareholders, are the owners of the company. The ordinary shareholders have **no right** to receive a dividend, and the size of the payment will depend upon company policy and profitability.

- Share premium

Whenever a company goes public its shares are **sold to investors** who will be able to buy and sell them on a recognised stock market. The existing owners are unlikely to sell the new shares at their nominal value because this price would fail to take account of the assets and profitability of the company. As a result the shares are sold for more than their nominal value and this is how the **share premium** arises. The difference between the nominal value and the flotation price is placed in a capital reserve and shown in the Balance Sheet as share premium.

• Capital reserves and revenue reserves

The Companies Acts distinguish between two types of reserves: capital reserves and revenue reserves. **Capital** reserves may **not** be used for paying dividends. A good example of such a reserve is a share premium and revaluation reserve, when fixed assets have increased in value, often as a result of inflation.

Revenue reserves may be used to **pay dividends**. The Profit and Loss Account balance shown in the Balance Sheet is a good example. When a company has paid its Corporation Tax, and transferred profits to its reserves, the balance of any profits left may be paid to the shareholders as dividend. Often the sum of money left would not be enough to pay a round sum to all shareholders and so a small surplus is left. This is kept in the business and shown as a reserve in the Balance Sheet under the heading "Profit and Loss Account". The company may use this reserve to make up shareholder dividends in the event of a fall in profits brought about by adverse trading conditions.

Reports appended to the Accounts

Directors' report

By law the directors' report must disclose the following information:

(a) A **review of the business** which describes the principal **activities** of the company and any **changes** which have occurred during the year

(b) The company's **after tax profit**, the amount of money transferred to **reserves** and the recommended **dividend** which will be paid to shareholders

(c) The **market value** of **land and buildings**

(d) Any **donations given to political parties** or **charitable institutions**

(e) Details of any **significant changes** to the company's **fixed assets**

(f) If the company employs more than 250 people, its policy with regard to **recruitment, employment** and **training** of **disabled people**

(g) The **names** of the directors during the last financial year and the number of **shares and debenture** stock which they hold

(h) Details of any important **events** which have happened since the end of the financial year

(i) Details of the company's **future developments**

(j) The company's **research and development programmes**

(k) How the firm has tried to introduce, maintain or develop **employee information, consultation, involvement** and **company performance** during the year

(l) Information about the arrangements for securing the **health, safety and welfare at work** of employees and other people connected with the work activities of their employees.

Auditors' report

The company directors may appoint the auditors for the first time when a company begins operations, but subsequently it is the shareholders who appoint the auditors. The usual procedure is for the board of directors to recommend the appointment of a firm of auditors and for the shareholders to express their approval by voting in favour (or against) the motion.

The auditor's report will confirm that the accounts have been audited in accordance with the Auditing Standards, and that they give a **true and fair view** of the affairs of the company at a said date. The words "true and fair" have never been defined, either by Parliament or the courts, but the best explanation of the term is that they are without bias, as we saw in Chapter 2.

The changing nature of company accounting requirements

The precise format of company accounts changes as new legislation or Financial Reporting Standards seek to clarify or explain in greater depth financial information which is of interest to shareholders and other business users. This chapter has sought to explain the key elements of company accounts and the main regulations which company directors must abide by. More information can be found on this by referring to relevant Companies Acts and Financial Reporting Standards.

Study tasks

1 The Croeso Hotel has just finished its financial year. What information must be disclosed in the company's Profit and Loss Account?

2 What information must Sarah and Kate show in their Directors' report?

3 From the following information prepare the Croeso Hotel Trading Profit and Loss account; and Balance Sheet

Croeso Hotel: Trial Balance for Year 2

	Dr £	Cr £
Sales		210,000
Share capital ord. £1 Shares		140,000
Mortgage		40,000
Creditors		20,000
Discount received		500
Interest received		200
Bank loan		10,000
Opening stock	35,000	
Hotel	140,000	
Fixtures and fittings	20,000	
Purchases	80,000	
Debtors	44,000	
Wages	70,000	
Insurance	3,000	
Heating and lighting	6,000	
Postage and telephone	1,000	
Gardening	2,000	
Audit fee	1,700	
Rates	6,000	
Motor expenses	2,000	
Advertising	1,500	
Printing and stationery	3,500	
Repairs and renewals	5,000	
	420,700	420,700

Closing stock £15,000

4 Using the information from Question 3, prepare the Croeso Hotel's Profit and Loss Account as it would appear in a published corporate report.

5 Sarah and Kate are considering selling some shares to employees who have worked for the company for 2 years. The nominal price of the ordinary shares is £1 but their market value is in excess of this. State how the proceeds from the sale of these shares would be shown in the accounts, explaining the difference between a capital and a revenue reserve as part of the answer.

6 As Kate and Sarah are the owners of the Croeso Hotel business, what information shown in the company accounts will be particularly relevant in determing the value of their shares?

11 Preparing Cash Flow Statements

The need to generate cash

The long-term survival of any business depends on its ability to **generate cash** from its main trading activities. Although it can raise money by borrowing or by selling additional shares there is a limit to the amount of capital that can be financed from outside sources. The same is true of asset disposals. Although selling fixed assets raises cash there is a limit to the number which can be sold before it affects the firm's trading and profitability.

A downturn in economic activity concentrates managers', investors' and analysts' minds on a firm's ability to generate cash. The Profit and Loss Account and Balance Sheet do not show the changes in the business's cash position during the last financial year. A look at the Balance Sheet, whilst showing the amount of cash a business **has**, does not show how it has been **generated**. It is this information which is important and is best shown by preparing a Cash Flow Statement.

In Britain Cash Flow Statements are relatively new, being introduced in 1991 following the publication of the first Financial Reporting Standard on Cash Flow Accounting. Prior to this firms had prepared a Source and Application Statement which showed the changes in net working capital but not the change in its cash position, which was a major limitation.

How trading affects a firm's cash position

- A firm **generates** cash by **selling** its products or services. It **spends** its cash by **paying** for materials, labour and the overheads which it incurs in its day-to-day trading activities. Cash can also be received by **borrowing** or by **selling fixed assets**. These are the only sources of cash available.

- Cash will also be used to **purchase** additional fixed assets, meet **interest payments**, and pay **taxes** and **dividends** to shareholders.

- Any spending of cash is called an **application of funds**, and must be paid for by using the assets of the business to generate cash. In theory the cash generated from the assets will equal the cash paid to creditors and owners.

- If a firm is having to increase its short-term borrowings to meet the cash payments to creditors and owners then a cash flow statment will reveal how this situation has come about.

Preparing a Cash Flow Statement

The Cash Flow Statement is constructed by using the information contained in a firm's last two years' annual accounts. Look at the Balance Sheet for Ice House, a ski manufacturer, in Figure 11.1.

Figure 11.1   Ice House: Balance Sheets as at end of Year 1 and 2

		Year 1 £		Year 2 £
Fixed Assets				
Premises		340,000		420,000
Plant and machinery		40,000		60,000
Motor vehicles		–		8,000
		380,000		488,000
Current Assets				
Stock	60,000		108,000	
Debtors	44,000		84,000	
Bank	32,000		52,000	
	136,000		244,000	
Current Liabilities				
Creditors	36,000		40,000	

continued over

	Year 1 £	Year 2 £
	100,000	204,000
Net Assets	480,000	692,000
Financed by		
Ordinary share capital	480,000	520,000
Profit and Loss	–	112,000
Long-term loans		60,000
Capital employed	480,000	692,000

Sources and application of funds

Before preparing a Cash Flow Statement it is good practice as a first step to record the sources and application of funds during the year. This is done by looking at the information contained in the Profit and Loss Account and Balance Sheet. The Profit and Loss Account will show the retained profit and so this must be a **source** of funds. The majority of the information will be contained in the Balance Sheet. By looking at the two years it is possible to see the changes which have occurred, as in Figure 11.2.

Figure 11.2   Ice House: sources and application of funds

Sources of cash	£
Increase in retained earnings	112
Increase in share capital	40
Increase in creditors	4
Increase in long-term loans	60
Total Sources	216
Application of Cash	
Increase in plant	20
Increase in premises	80
Increase in motor vehicles	8
Increase in stock	48
Increase in debtors	40
Increase in bank deposits	20
Total Applications	216

The sources of funds must equal the uses, and so once these two sets of figures agree a Cash Flow Statement can be prepared, as in Figure 11.3.

Figure 11.3   Ice House: Cash Flow Statement for year ended Year 2

	£	£
Cash flow from operating activities	28,000	
Investing activities Payments to acquire tangible fixed assets		(108,000)
		80,000
Financing		
Issue of ord. shares	40,000	
Long-term loans	60,000	
		100,000
Increase in cash		20,000
Reconciliation of operating profit to net cash flow investment From operating activities		
Operating profit		112,000
Increase in stock		(48,000)
Increase in debtors		(40,000)
Increase in creditors		4,000
Net cash flow from operating activities		28,000

	Year 1 £	Year 2 £	Change in Year £
Increase in cash and cash equivalents			
Cash at bank and in Hand	52,000	32,000	20,000

What does the Cash Flow Statement show?

Use of cash generated

This statement shows how a firm has **generated** and **used** its cash during the year. We can see that Ice House has used its cash to finance more fixed assets, stock, and debtors and has increased its cash balances. By holding more stocks and allowing its debtors to increase the business is tying up more of its cash resources in these two current assets.

It may seem strange that an increase in cash is treated as an **application** of funds, but the reason is that the money has not been used. Only once withdrawals are made does it become a source. Cash balances are therefore treated the same way as the other two current assets – stock and debtors.

Financing company spending

Whatever money has been spent on acquiring additional assets it must have been financed. There are only **three** ways that this can be done: **generating profits**, by **raising additional finance** from an outside source, and by **selling fixed assets**. All of these methods will increase a firm's cash. Ice House has increased its sources of cash by selling more shares, and increasing long-term debt. The amount of money owed to creditors has also increased and the rest of the money has been generated through profitable trading.

The importance of cash flow

Although there has been considerable debate in the accountancy profession about Cash Flow Statements, they have a long history. At the turn of the century the American railways companies were preparing statements showing the changes in current assets and current liabilities during a financial year.These early managers had realised the importance of cash, and seen that a profitable businesses can still be forced into liquidation once it is unable to generate sufficient cash to meet its liabilities.

Study tasks

1 Prepare a short report to Sarah and Kate, outlining how the Croeso Hotel could be profitable, and yet short of cash.

2 Identify **three** ways in which the Croeso Hotel can increase its cash resources.

3 Explain why the information shown in the Croeso Hotel's Cash Flow Statement would be useful to:

> • creditors
> • investors
> • managers
> • employees

4 State which of the following are a source, and which an application, of funds for the Croeso Hotel:

	Source	Application
(a) Increase in cash		
(b) Purchase of fixed assets		
(c) Depreciation		
(d) Repayment of bank loan		
(e) Profit		
(f) Increase in stock		
(g) Share premium		
(h) Increase in creditors		
(i) Issue of ordinary shares		
(j) Decrease in debtors		

5 Kate is a shareholder in her brother's bakery business and has just received the annual accounts. Unfortunately a Cash Flow Statement has not been prepared and so you have been asked to produce one from the firm's last two sets of annual accounts.

The Bakery: Balance Sheet as at 31 December Year 2

		Year 1 £		Year 2 £
Fixed assets				
Premises		120,000		160,000
Fixtures and fittings		20,000		34,000
		140,000		194,000
Current assets				
Stock	30,000		54,000	
Debtors	22,000		42,000	
Bank	16,000		26,000	
	68,000		122,000	
Less current liabilities				
Creditors	18,000		20,000	
Working capital		50,000		102,000
Net assets		190,000		296,000
Financed by				
Ordinary share capital		190,000		210,000
Profit and loss		–		56,000
Long term loans				30,000
		190,000		296,000

6 Write a memo to Kate explaining the figures in your Cash Flow Statement, and what importance they have for the business at The Bakery.

Part II
Applying Management Accounting Techniques for Planning, Controlling and Decision Making in a Business

12 Cost Behaviour and Control

The importance of cost and management accounting

So far, we have considered financial accounting, which is concerned with recording all historical financial transactions and presenting them to shareholders and other interested parties, usually in the form of a set of annual accounts. As a result, many people see the role of financial accounting as that of a steward who looks after and reports on the financial affairs of the business.

Whilst this information forms the bedrock of any accounting information system it is of limited use for day-to-day management planning and control. Cost accounting techniques were first developed in the United States to provide management with accounting information which would assist them in decision making. Unlike financial accounting there is no legal requirement to prepare management accounts, and the costs of doing so must be less than the benefits derived from them.

If a business is to trade profitably a number of decisions have to be made about the prices, the desired level of operating activity and the volume of sales needed to cover costs and make a profit. In the long term a business must be capable of generating sufficient revenue to cover costs, pay a return to the owners and leave sufficient profits for reinvestment.

Cost accounting terminology

What is a "cost"?

The word "cost" can be defined as the **expenditure incurred** in **producing goods** or **services**. This may not be just the actual money paid out, but can also include the cost foregone by deciding to spend the money in one way as opposed to another. As managers have to choose between different alternatives one can argue that this is really the true cost of any decision. This is usually referred to as the **opportunity cost**.

117

Cost unit

Cost accounting, like financial accounting, has its own set of terminology. All units of production or services provided are called **cost units**. In a hotel, a meal prepared in the kitchen would be called a cost unit, whereas in a brewery the term would be used to describe a barrel of beer. If all the costs involved were **direct** it would be relatively easy to calculate the cost unit. The problem is that some expenses, such as hotel insurance, are not directly related to the costs of providing food but are still related to the overall overheads of running the business. As these indirect costs cannot be directly applied to the cost unit they must be **apportioned** to them instead.

Apportionment of overheads

The word "apportioned" in accounting means **shared**. Overheads such as rent and insurance must therefore be apportioned. A stately home which is open to the public must insure the buildings and contents as well as having cover for visitors and employees. This cost should not be borne just by the exhibition rooms but by all the facilities being offered. By dividing up the insurance cost amongst all of the other attractions, such as the gift shop and restaurant, the insurance can be apportioned to each department.

Allocation of costs

It must be remembered that cost apportionment owes its origin to manufacturing industry and that therefore not all methods are appropriate to service sector industries. Two popular methods of allocating costs are according to the physical size of a particular department or according to its revenue. In all cases of allocating costs the method must take account of the **activity**. In a stately home, the insurance cost could be allocated according to the number of visitors who attend each part of the house. This method, however, would not be suitable for Ice House, where the main activity is the labour involved in making skis. In the Ice House's case the best method would be to apportion overheads such as insurance according to the labour hours taken to make each pair of skis.

Direct and indirect costs

By allocating all direct and indirect costs to individual cost units management know the precise costs of making goods or providing services. By classifying expenditure into direct and indirect it is possible to see what the main costs are of making a product or providing a service. A garden centre which sells hanging baskets would classify the container, soil and plants as direct costs, together with the labour charge involved in making up the baskets. Other costs not directly traceable to this work, such as heating the greenhouse, would be classified as indirect because they are not so easily identifiable at the **unit level**.

Cost classification and behaviour

Once costs have been classified as direct and indirect they can be further separated according to their nature, function or behaviour.

Nature

This is the technical term used to define what the **cost is**. For instance, the food which is prepared in the kitchen is a separate cost from the cost of sending the linen to the laundry. By classifying costs according to their nature management can see how much money is being spent on certain items, and **comparisons** can be made between one time period and the next.

Function

Businesses often divide their work into departments such as marketing, finance and personnel so that costs can be allocated to each of these functions. A hotel, for example, is usually split into front of house, accommodation, food and beverage and administration. By doing this the costs can be allocated to each area, thereby providing management with accurate cost details of each part of the business.

Cost behaviour

Important though the last two categories are they take no account of how costs change with different levels of **operating capacity**. In order to meet this need costs can be classified as being **fixed, variable** or **semi-variable** in relation to different levels of business activity. We shall now look at each of these.

Fixed costs

This is the name given to those costs which are **not affected by different operating levels**. If a health farm has to pay £20,000 a year in rent, that sum is fixed regardless of the level of occupancy in the establishment. This means that the amount paid will not be reduced or increased by any changes in the number of people booking a stay at the health farm.

Total fixed costs

We have already seen that a fixed cost does not alter according to the level of activity. It can be represented as a graph where it is shown as a straight line, reflecting the fact that regardless of the operating capacity this cost must be paid in full (see Figure 12.1).

Figure 12.1   Total fixed costs

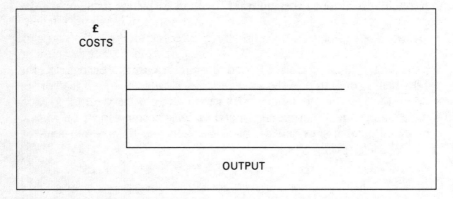

Fixed cost per unit

Although the fixed costs remain the same in total the proportion borne by **each unit of output** or **customer** will change as the firm experiences different levels of activity. Graphically this can be presented as in Figure 12.2.

Figure 12.2   Fixed cost per unit

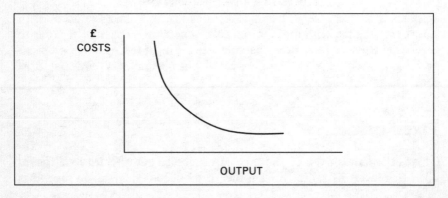

If a residential management centre has 100 rooms and pays £1,000 rent a week, then this fixed cost must be spread over the number of rooms. If all rooms were occupied each week then the fixed cost per room at that level would be £10. If only 50 rooms were let then the fixed cost per room would double to £20. This shows that although the rent remains fixed in total, the unit cost per room alters with different levels of occupancy.

Variable costs

These are costs which **are affected by changes in the level of activity**. If the health farm had no guests there would be no need to prepare any meals for the restaurant. In such a case the firm could save the food costs involved and any direct labour not required in the kitchen. The more guests staying and eating, the greater the food bill. This type of cost is described as being "variable" because any increase or decrease in activity will directly affect the **total cost** of providing the service (see Figure 12.3 and 12.4.

Figure 12.3   Total variable cost

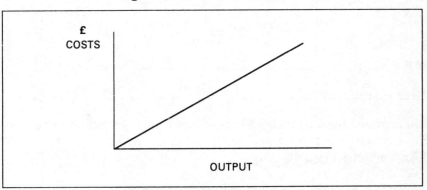

Figure 12.4   Unit variable cost

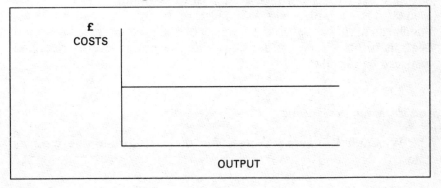

In accounting, the unit variable cost is assumed to be the same because bulk buying discounts are ignored.

Semi-variable costs

Not all costs can be immediately separated into fixed or variable elements because they contain a **mixture of both**. The telephone bill is a good example because the rental cost is fixed while each telephone call increases the total bill and is therefore a variable cost. In practice semi-variable costs can be divided into a **fixed** or **variable** category, depending upon which part is the main proportion of the cost (see Figure 12.5).

Figure 12.5   Semi-variable cost

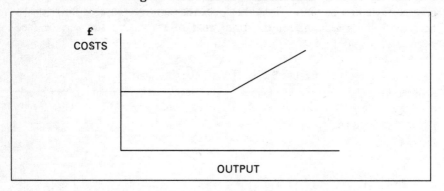

Managing costs

Separation of costs into fixed and variable elements

A firm's fixed costs must be paid regardless of the level of activity whereas the variable costs will increase in total as activity rises. Management must be able to separate their costs into these two elements before a range of decisions about operating levels, prices and costs can be calculated.

The Windmill Restaurant

The Windmill Restaurant's costs for the last six months were as follows:

	Jul	Aug	Sep	Oct	Nov	Dec
Covers	6,000	7,500	8,000	6,900	5,900	4,000
	£	£	£	£	£	£
Food costs	8,400	10,500	11,200	9,660	8,260	5,600
Overheads	12,500	13,625	14,000	13,175	12,425	11,000

Arranged in this format the information is of limited use for decision making, for management need to know how their costs **alter** with **different levels of activity**. This can only be worked out by separating the costs into their fixed and variable elements.

The food costs must be a **variable cost** because the more food that the restaurant serves, the greater the total cost. In accounting although the total cost increases the cost per unit stays the same: by dividing the number of servings each month into the food cost the cost of the food can be found, and if the cost per unit remains constant we will have proved it to be a variable cost:

	Jul	Aug	Sep	Oct	Nov	Dec
Covers	6,000	7,500	8,000	6,900	5,900	4,000
	£	£	£	£	£	£
Food costs	8,400	10,500	11,200	9,660	8,260	5,600
Cost per meal	£1.40	£1.40	£1.40	£1.40	£1.40	£1.40

The overhead cost increases as the restaurant serves more customers. If they were a fixed cost then the overhead cost would remain the same. The fact that it increases means that the overheads must be made up of fixed and variable costs. These must now be separated. This is done by dividing the **change in cost** by the **change in activity** so that the variable cost of the overhead can be calculated:

	Cost £	Activity
Highest	14,000	8,000
Lowest	11,000	4,000
Change in cost/activity	3,000	4,000

By dividing cost by activity we can calculate the variable cost of the overhead:

Cost/Activity = £3,000/4,000 = 75p

If the variable cost of the overhead is multipled by the number of servings the total cost of the variable overhead can be calculated. If this figure is subtracted from the total overhead the fixed costs of the firm will be known:

	£	£	£	£	£	£
Overheads	12,500	13,625	14,000	13,175	12,425	11,000
Less Variable cost x output	4,500	5,625	6,000	5,175	4,425	3,000
Fixed costs	8,000	8,000	8,000	8,000	8,000	8,000

The restaurant management now know that their variable costs are £1.40 for food and 75p for variable overheads and that their fixed costs are £8,000 regardless of the number of guests served.

Another method of separating costs into their fixed and variable elements is by plotting a firm's costs and output on graph paper in order to calculate the fixed and variable costs.

Trimmer's Bar

The number of meals served by Trimmer's Bar for the last six months and their associated costs are as follows:

Month	Meals	Total costs £
Jan	8,000	15,000
Feb	6,000	14,000
Mar	12,000	21,000
Apr	10,800	18,000
May	13,600	22,000
Jun	9,200	18,000

By plotting costs and output levels as in Figure 12.6 a scatter graph can be produced. By drawing a "line of best fit" it is possible to calculate the fixed and variable costs. The line of best fit cuts the cost axis at £8,000 and this then shows the bar's fixed costs. Any cost above this level is **variable** and therefore explains why total costs increase with output.

Figure 12.6   Trimmer's Bar: fixed and variable costs

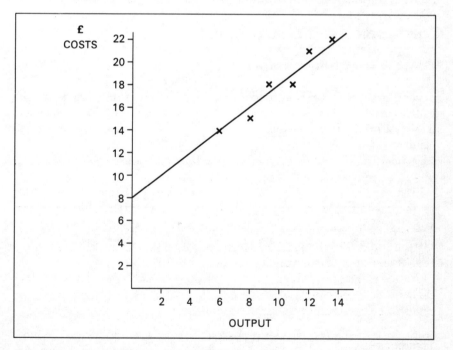

From Figure 12.6 we can see that the fixed costs are £8,000, and from this the variable costs can be calculated:

	£
Total costs at 16,000 meals	24,000
Less fixed costs	8,000
Total variable costs	16,000

If the total variable costs are divided by output the variable cost per unit can be calculated.

$$\frac{\text{Total variable cost}}{\text{Output}} \quad \frac{£16,000}{16,000} \quad = £1 \text{ per unit}$$

The break even chart

What the chart tells management

Once the costs have been separated management know how much **revenue must be earned** to cover both the variable and fixed costs of making a product or providing a service. The break even chart is a very useful tool because it is able to present **two** pieces of information at the same time. It will show the **number of units** which must be sold and the **total sales volume** needed to cover all of the firm's costs.

Even though a firm has reached its break even (B/E) point it will still not be profitable. At this level of activity its total revenues will only **equal** costs. Nevertheless break even charts illustrating the profit or loss at different levels of output are a useful aid to management decision making.

Trimmer's Bar

With our cost figures, we can prepare the break even point for the bar. Before this can be done, we need information from the owners about the **number** of meals which they intend to sell, together with their **selling price**.

Cost and sales information

Let us assume that they intend to sell 14,000 meals in July at a selling price of £2 each.

We then need to know what figures we are going to present on our graph:

•	Fixed costs per annum	£8,000
•	Variable cost per unit	£1
•	Estimated sales per annum	14,000 meals
•	Selling price per meal	£2

Drawing the graph

This information can now be used to draw our graph and calculate the break even point (see Figure 12.7).

Figure 12.7   Trimmer's Bar: Break even chart

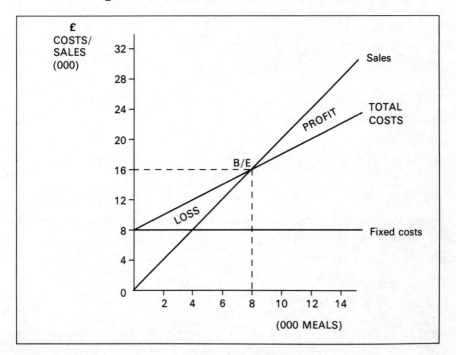

Figure 12.7 shows that Trimmer's break even point is either 8,000 meals or £16,000 sales.

Calculating break even point by a formula

We know that at Trimmer's Bar the selling price is £2 per meal and that the variable cost of each meal is £1. If the variable cost is subtracted from the selling price we can see that each meal sold **contributes £1 towards fixed costs**. Once this "contribution" has been calculated the break even point can be worked out by using a formula.

If the business needs to know how many units must be sold then the break even point is calculated by dividing the contribution into the fixed costs. The word "contribution" defines the **surplus which is left** once the variable costs have been deducted from the sales revenue. The concept is explained further in Chapter 13 but we can use it in our formula for calculating break even:

- The first step is to calculate the **unit contribution**

	£
Selling price	2
Less variable cost	1
Unit Contribution	1

$$\text{Break even} = \frac{\text{Fixed costs}}{\text{Contribution per meal}} \quad \frac{£8,000}{£1} = 8,000 \text{ units (meals)}$$

- Alternatively the break even point can be calculated in terms of **sales volume**.
  The formula is:

$$\text{Break Even} = \frac{\text{Total sales value} \times \text{Fixed costs}}{\text{Total contribution}}$$

- We can now use our Trimmer's Bar figures to calculate the **total contribution**:

	£
Total sales	28,000
Less total variable cost	14,000
Total contribution	14,000

$$\frac{£28,000 \times £8,000}{£14,000} = £16,000$$

Limitations of break even analysis

Although in theory the break even point is relatively easy to calculate, a number of assumptions are made which may or may not hold in practice. The firm's break even point will alter if any of the following events happen.

(1) The break even model assumes that costs and sales increase in **straight lines** (i.e. are linear). This may not always be so. If costs are not linear with volume then the firm may move **in and out of a break even** position as sales increase.

(2) An assumption is also made that production and sales are **in balance**. In the tourism, hospitality and leisure industries this is likely to be the situation because of the nature of the business. In manufacturing industry sales sometimes exceed production, and this will inevitably affect the break even point.

(3) The **time scale** is important. If the firm's sales are quicker or slower than expected, the break even point will be affected.

There is a danger that management may rely too heavily on a given break even point when in fact it is no longer applicable. Any of the above limitations will alter the break even point, as will unanticipated levels of inflation. Unless the firm's costs are amended to reflect these changes there is a real problem that a loss will be made because insufficient contribution is being earned to cover the unforeseen costs.

Break even as a management tool

In practice it is sometimes difficult to separate costs according to their behaviour because increases in volume will in the long run make **all costs variable**, and this will alter the break even point. Whilst it is important to recognise these limitations, the break even concept is still useful for planning, decision making and setting operating targets.

Study tasks

1   State which of the following costs at the Croeso Hotel are direct, and which are indirect:

Cost	Direct	Indirect
(a) Food		
(b) Insurance		
(c) Chef's wages		
(d) Head Waiter's wages		
(e) Gas for cooking		
(f) Alcohol		
(g) Rent		
(h) Supervisor's wages		

2   Hugh Roberts, the Head Chef at the Croeso Hotel, has supplied you with the following information. Calculate the variable cost of each meal they have served.

Covers	1,500	2,600	3,200	1,992	4,300	5180
	£	£	£	£	£	£
Food costs	9,375	16,250	20,000	12,450	26,875	32,375

3   Sarah and Kate are considering holding a firework evening at the hotel. The costs of the fireworks would be £2,000. Calculate how the fixed costs would change if the following number of people came to the event:

No. of visitors	Fixed cost per guest £
0	
10	
50	
100	
150	
200	
250	
500	
750	
1,000	

4   Sarah and Kate are also considering holding a fashion show for local Welsh Woollen Mills. The hotel will provide a buffet lunch and tickets will sell for £15 a head. The maximum number of guests which the Croeso Hotel could cater for is 300. From the following information calculate the costs, sales and profits at 50%, 60%, 70%, 80% 90% and 100% level of operating capacity:

Variable costs per guest	£
Food costs	9
Direct labour	3
Drink	2
Fixed costs	
Overheads	900

5   During the last 4 months the Croeso Hotel's Valley View Bar has incurred the following costs. Calculate the bar's fixed and variable costs:

	May £	Jun £	Jul £	Aug £
Bar food costs	3,675	4,200	5,040	6,510
Alcohol	2,485	2,840	3,408	4,402
Overheads	2,150	2,300	2,540	2,960
Customers	1,750	2,000	2,400	3,100

6   The Croeso Hotel's Victoria Restaurant's costs for the last six months are shown below. Calculate the restaurant's fixed, variable costs and profits if each meal sells for £18:

	Jan	Feb	Mar	Apr	May	Jun
Covers	800	750	1,400	1,800	2,200	2,700
	£	£	£	£	£	£
Food	5,920	5,550	10,360	13,320	16,280	19,980
Alcohol	2,480	2,325	4,340	5,580	6,820	8,370
Labour	2,000	1,875	3,500	4,500	5,500	6,750
Overheads	4,120	4,050	4,960	5,520	6,080	6,780

13 Cost Analysis and Decision Making

The importance of identifying costs

Management need to be able to identify all of the costs involved in running a business. A conference centre must be able to work out the costs of providing facilities before deciding its pricing strategy, for example. We saw in Chapter 12 that costs can be classified according to their behaviour. For the business to make a profit all costs, be they fixed or variable, must be **covered**.

Methods of apportioning costs

In Chapter 12 we saw that costs must be **allocated** or **apportioned** to a cost centre on the basis of how easily identifiable they are with a particular department.

Costs can be said to be either **direct** or **indirect**. If they are direct it is easy to allocate them to cost centres because they are related to producing the goods or providing the services. The problem arises with how to deal with indirect costs. These, by their very nature, are not easily traceable, and so they must be **apportioned**.

There are three main methods of apportioning costs which relate to the **amount** produced, the **hours** worked and the **machine hours** used. Management must use a method of apportionment which is a fair reflection of the overheads incurred.

Honey Ices: calculation of overhead absorption rate

Honey Ices Limited has fixed overheads of £30,000 per quarter. Each quarter the firm produce 180,000 litres of ice cream which takes 6,000 labour hours and 1,500 machine hours.

132

- **Output method**

$$\frac{\text{Total overhead for cost centre}}{\text{No. of cost units produced}} = \frac{£30,000}{180,000} = \text{17p approx. per litre of ice cream}$$

- **Labour hour method**

$$\frac{\text{Total overheads for cost centre}}{\text{No. of labour hours}} = \frac{£30,000}{6,000 \text{ hours}} = \frac{£5}{\text{per hour of labour}}$$

- **Machine hour method**

$$\frac{\text{Total overhead for cost centre}}{\text{No. of Machine Hours}} = \frac{£30,000}{1,500 \text{ hours}} = \frac{£20}{\text{per machine hour}}$$

Product costing methods and techniques

There are two main methods of costing a product or service: **absorption costing** and **marginal costing**. Technically it is not correct to call marginal costing a method because it only considers the variable costs.

Absorption costing

This method calculates the **total cost** of providing a service or making a product. As a result absorption costing is sometimes referred to as "full costing", because it includes both the fixed and variable cost. The figures for Infotech and the Croeso Hotel show how this method can be used to calculate the cost of providing a function in a hotel.

Infotech: quotation for dinner and dance

Infotech, a local company, intends to invite its sales staff and customers to a special evening. The company has asked for quotes from a number of hotels including the Croeso Hotel, for the cost of providing a three-course dinner and dance. The company intend to invite 150 people. The Croeso Hotel's estimated costs are:

	£
Food costs £12 per meal × 150 guests	1,800
Direct labour 40 hours at £5 per hour	200
Wine and beverages	1,200
Variable overheads	200
Share of fixed overheads	2,500
Absorption cost	5,900

Relevant costs

If the Croeso Hotel is to make a profit it must charge more than £5,900 for providing the function. Whilst these amounts must be covered for the business to make a profit, simply considering the total costs is not always the best way of controlling them. The conference centre already has to meet fixed costs of £2,500: these will have to be paid whether or not the function takes place. The other costs, which amount to £3,400, will be incurred only if the function goes ahead. As a result the only costs which are relevant to a decision are those which are affected by it. The relevant cost in this example is the **£3,400 variable cost**.

Marginal costing

The Infotech quotation

Marginal costing only considers the **variable** or **marginal** cost of producing a product or providing a service. We can now calculate the marginal cost of Infotech's function evening:

	£
Food costs £12 per meal × 150 guests	1,800
Direct labour 40 hours at £5 per hour	200
Wine and beverages	1,200
Variable overheads	200
Marginal Cost	3,400

Value to management

The main benefit of using marginal costing is that it helps management in their role of planning and decision making. By presenting the information in this way decisions can be made about pricing strategies, output levels and predicted profits.

If management are to achieve their objectives they must know how the firm's costs will alter with any change in activity. We have already seen that within a certain range of activity the fixed costs will remain the same, and so it is the **variable** costs which will account for the difference in total cost. As a result it will usually be the variable or marginal cost which is most applicable to the decision, as it was for the Croeso Hotel here.

Contribution and fixed costs

The costings for the Infotech function show the marginal cost to be £3,400. Any selling price above this amount will generate what accountants call "contribution". Contribution must not be regarded as profit, because the fixed costs have not been accounted for, but it will help towards **paying them**. This is an important concept for decision making because even if the contribution earned from a sale is not sufficient to meet all the fixed costs it will still help to pay part of them.

In the hotel industry accommodation is perishable because an unoccupied room today cannot be sold twice tomorrow. The same principle applies when selling airline or theatre tickets. In such cases, management should aim to maximise the contribution by discounting the selling price with the aim of increasing the **number of customers** and **total revenues**.

Differential cost

Although costs can be categorised as being either fixed or variable over a specified level of output this separation is not appropriate because most management decisions will involve a change in operating levels. In such cases, management must assess which costs are relevant to the decision being made so that the change in cost, usually referred to as the "differential cost", can be calculated. If the food cost of one meal at the Croeso Hotel is £15 per head while for another meal it is £20, then the extra £5 in cost is the **differential cost**.

Relevant cost

Whenever a decision involves an inflow or outflow of money, it is said to be a "relevant cost". Whenever a decision is being made, as we have seen, only the relevant costs should be considered. These are usually the **additional variable costs**, but in some cases the firm may incur additional fixed costs as well.

Non-relevant cost

The following costs are **not relevant** when making a decision:

(**1**) Money already spent on **past costs**

(**2**) Non-cash costs such as **depreciation**

(**3**) Overheads which have **already been absorbed**

(**4**) Decisions already taken which have committed the business to **future expenditure**.

Future costs and revenues

It is important to remember that once money has been spent it cannot be used again and so only **future** costs and revenues are really relevant when making decisions.

Financial aspects of short-term decision making

Whenever decisions are being made about altering output levels in the short term it is the **relevant costs** which are important. Marginal costing methods make these changes in costs immediately apparent: if the fixed costs do not alter in the short term then the only relevant costs are the variable or marginal ones.

The key to effective decision making is how profits are affected by changes in **sales volumes**. The figures for Ruskin's Wine Bar and Munchie's Restaurant show how marginal costing techniques can assist management.

Ruskin's Wine Bar: deciding which products to sell

Ruskin's Wine Bar is considering stocking a new French wine. The management have drawn up a short list of three wines and then ranked them by contribution (see Figures 13.1 and 13.2).

Figure 13.1   Ruskin's Wine Bar: short list of wines to be stocked

Product (wine)	Selling price £	Purchase price £	Estimated sales (Units)
Vin du Pays	8.00	5.00	500
Blanc de Blanc	15.00	9.00	400
Bordeaux	12.00	7.00	300

Figure 13.2   Ruskin's Wine Bar: ranking of wines by contribution

Product (wine)	Selling price £	Marginal cost £	Contribution per unit £
Vin du Pays	8.00	5.00	3.00
Blanc de Blanc	15.00	9.00	6.00
Bordeaux	12.00	7.00	5.00

Note: The purchase price here is the marginal or variable cost.

By ranking the wines in this way it can be seen which wines will generate the highest unit and total contribution for Ruskin's. If the wine bar is to optimise its profits it must maximise its contribution, and this will be achieved by stocking Blanc de Blanc because it has the **highest unit and total contribution**.

Munchie's Restaurant: limiting factors

Whilst a firm should always seek to increase its contribution a simple ranking of the possible contribution to be earned may not always be appropriate. In some situations different times will be spent making a product, or only a limited number of units can be sold. These restrictions are called **limiting factors**, and the aim in such cases is to maximise the contribution once the limiting factor has been taken into account.

Munchie's Restaurant is considering its lunchtime menu. The manager is undecided as to whether to offer customers a meat or fish main course. The relevant costs are shown in Figure 13.3, and the choice of menu based on contribution in Figure 13.4.

Figure 13.3   Munchie's Restaurant: relevant costs

	Meat £	Fish £
Food cost	6	9
Direct labour	8	12
(4 hours)		
Variable overheads	2	2
Marginal cost	16	23

The meat menu sells for £30 per person and the fish for £38. Which menu would maximise the restaurant's profits?

Figure 13.4   Munchie's Restaurant: choice of menu based on contribution

	Meat £	Fish £
Selling price	30	38
Less marginal costs	16	23
Contribution ÷	14	15
Labour hours	2	3
Contribution per		
labour hour	7	5

Labour is the limiting factor for Munchie's, and therefore it is not appropriate to choose the fish menu because it makes the larger contribution. The important element is the contribution **earned per hour**, and once this criterion is applied the restaurant will maximise its contribution by using the meat menu.

Covering costs to achieve profitability

These business transactions all demonstrate how marginal costing techniques can assist management decision making when fixed costs remain unaltered. The fixed costs can only be ignored if they are not relevant to the decision being taken: this means that they will neither increase or decrease once the decision has been made. If they were to alter they would be a relevant cost and would have to be considered. Finally it must always be remembered that in the long term **all costs**, both fixed and variable, must be covered if the business is to achieve its goal of being profitable.

Study tasks

1   The Croeso Hotel's Victoria Restaurant has fixed overheads of £70,000 per quarter. Each quarter, the restaurant serves 40,000 meals, which takes 3,500 labour hours and 1,200 oven hours.
How can the Croeso Hotel apportion its costs? Calculate the overhead absorption rate using

> (**a**) The output method
> (**b**) Labour hours
> (**c**) Oven hours.

2   Sarah and Kate are considering purchasing an ice-making machine for the Croeso Hotel's Valley View Bar. Last year they invested £4,000 in new bar furniture and £2,000 in a new carpet. Kate is reluctant to spend more money on the bar this year and has cited the £6,000 already spent as an argument against investing any more money.

> (**a**) What are the relevant costs of this investment, and why should only relevant costs be considered when making investment decisions?
> (**b**) What are the opportunity costs?
> (**c**) What are the sunk costs?

3 Calculate the contribution earned from the sale of the following main course meals in the Croeso Hotel's Victoria Restaurant:

	Beef £	Duck £	Chicken £
Selling price	14	12	10
Food cost	6	5	4
Direct labour	3	2	2
Variable overheads	2	1	1

4 Monica Petrocelli, the part-time pastry chef, is considering making either a Black Forest Gateau or a sherry trifle for a company dinner party. The costs and revenues are shown below:

	Gateau £	Trifle £
Selling price per portion	5	4.50
Food cost	2	1.50
Labour	1.50	1
Labour hours	2	1

(a) Calculate the contribution earned from the sale of the gateau and the trifle.

(b) Which one should Monica make, and why?

5 The Croeso Hotel's Health Centre has a Gymnasium, Sauna and Swimming Pool. The cost is £8 per visit and this allows a guest to use any of the facilities. The marginal costs have been calculated at £4.50 per visit. Calculate the break even point if the Centre's fixed costs are £15,000 per annum and it has 250 customers per week.

6 The Croeso Hotel has been asked to arrange a barbecue for Delmonds, a local electronics company. 200 people would attend and the company are prepared to pay £9 a head. Sarah has estimated that the fixed costs of the evening would be £800. The other costs are shown below:

Per head	£
Food	2.50
Labour	1.25
Drinks	2.00

(a) Calculate the contribution earned from each guest

(b) Calculate the break even point for the evening

(c) Prepare a Profit and Loss Account in marginal cost format showing the profit or loss which the Croeso Hotel would earn from the function.

14 Managing Budgets

Targets for performance

Most businesses set targets for performance before the start of each financial year. Management may aim to increase sales, reduce costs and increase profits so that over time the organisation is able to raise the return on its capital employed (see Chapter 18). If any of these objectives are to be achieved, plans must be made which will turn these ambitions into reality. The setting of **budgets** for the functional areas of a hotel, which would include food and beverage, front of house, and accommodation, would enable management to see how the corporate objectives would affect all aspects of the business.

Budgetary control

Introducing the system: staff consultation

A firm may be considering introducing a system of budgetary control for the first time, or it may be continuing with an existing one. In either case it is important for all of the staff to be involved in the process. If they are not consulted, or if staff feel it is a ritual which happens once a year, the firm will fail to benefit from budgetary control. Unfortunately in many organisations staff are asked to prepare budgets which are then amended by Head Office, usually without consultation, often leaving the work-force demoralised. There is then a danger that when the budgets are prepared they are deliberately inflated so as to take account of cuts which may be imposed later. Needless to say, budgetary control will prove ineffective, and many of its benefits will be lost.

Establishing an effective system: the Budget Committee

Budgets should turn corporate plans into practice, but before this can happen senior management must determine the firm's **strategic objectives** for the next financial period. Once this has been completed work can begin on the budgetary process itself. The first task is to establish a Budget Committee which will usually be chaired by an accountant. It will be the chair's task to ensure that everyone within the organisation knows how to prepare their budget, can meet the agreed deadlines, and understands the importance and benefits of such a system.

Functional budgets and Master Budget

Once the timetable has been agreed the functional budgets can be prepared. The **Sales Budget** should always be produced first because many of the others cannot be prepared until the estimated level of **sales** and **units** has been calculated. When all the functional budgets have been agreed they can be consolidated into what is called the **Master Budget**. This is the technical term for a Budgeted Profit and Loss Account and Balance Sheet for the coming financial year. Many firms prepare a Master Budget for each quarter so that management can monitor and assess **actual** performance against **budgeted**. Only by doing this can **corrective action** be taken, thereby ensuring that events conform to the plan.

Budgets must be prepared for all of the **functional areas** of the business. The number and nature of these budgets will depend on the type of business, but **seven** will be common to organisations in the hospitality industry:

- Sales
- Food and beverage
- Labour
- Accommodation
- Administration
- Capital expenditure
- Cash

Sales budget

This will show the **anticipated level of sales** for the year. Firms will prepare the information in different ways – some may show sales by area, whilst others will show them by product or by the type of customer, e.g. domestic or foreign visitor.

Before this budget can be prepared account must be taken of the level of activity in the economy, political events and special events such as the

Olympic Games or a Trade Expo. In a recession, consumers are less likely to go on holiday or spend money on eating out in expensive restaurants: the more information of this kind a business has, the more realistic its sales forecast is likely to be. Any business has a great deal of information about **past sales**, **customers**, and **consumer seasonal purchasing trends** which should be analysed and incorporated into the Sales Budget.

Food and beverage budget

This will take account of the **planned level of sales** in the restaurant and bars. It cannot be prepared until the Sales Budget has been finalised.

Labour budget

The Labour Budget will show the number of staff needed to produce the **desired level of sales**, together with information relating to their wages and other employment costs such as pensions, employer's National Insurance contributions and any staff benefits such as subsidised meals and accommodation. The budget should also take account of the **efficiency** of the labour being used, and the different **grades** which will be required.

Accommodation budget

This will show the number of rooms which will be **operational** in a hotel during the next year. It must take account of rooms which will be closed for redecoration and refurbishment. In addition any plans for acquiring or disposing of property must be taken into consideration.

Administration budget

The Administration Budget should cover any expenditure which has **not been included** in the Labour and Capital Expenditure Budgets (see below). The budget will cover such costs as insurance, legal fees, audit charges, directors' fees, stationery, postage and telephone bills.

Capital expenditure budget

This will show the amount of money which the firm intends to spend on **additional fixed assets** during the coming financial year. The budget should show the planned expenditure on land and buildings, equipment, machinery and fixtures and fittings.

Cash budget

In the short term, profit and cash are not the same, although in the long term an **increase in profits** will lead to an **increase in cash**. The dilemma faced by all firms is that when goods are sold on credit no cash is received, although on paper the business will have made a profit so long as the selling price is higher than the cost price. If the business has too little cash to meet its current liabilities, even though it is profitable and has a high level of sales it may be forced into liquidation because it cannot meet its current financial obligations (see Chapter 17).

By drawing up a Cash Budget the firm is able to show all **predicted receipts and payments of cash**. Whilst some items such as the payment of rent will be known others, such as the receipt of cash from debtors, must be predicted. By adding up all receipts and deducting payments on a monthly basis the overall monthly cash position, be it positive or negative, can be forecast.

Once this task has been completed management will know if they have cash surpluses or deficits. Surpluses can be invested in interest-earning securities, thereby earning additional revenue for the business. Negative balances must be funded by obtaining outside finance, usually from banks in the form of an overdraft (see Chapter 19).

Coordination of budgets: limiting factors

Only once these budgets have been prepared will the firm know if the plans of one functional area are **compatible** with those of another. The Sales Budget for a scenic steam railway may show estimated sales of 5,000 passenger journeys whilst signalling facilities will only allow 4,000 journeys. In such a case management must accept the limitation, or seek to resolve the problem by investing in additional signalling facilities.

These limitations are referred to as "principal budget factors", and may be the result of either **internal** or **external** constraints. If the firm cannot sell all that it is capable of selling it is referred to as an external limiting factor. If it cannot produce all it could sell it is called an internal limiting factor. Butt's Brewery, for example, has the limiting factor problem shown in Figure 14.1 (on the following page).

This highlights Butt's Brewery's problem in not being able to brew enough beer to satisfy demand. Management must decide whether to accept this limitation and sell less than the market is willing to buy, or to increase capacity by investing in more plant and machinery.

Figure 14.1　Butt's Brewery: internal limiting factor

	Barrels
Potential sales	5,000
Productive capacity	4,300
Internal limiting factor	700

Preparation of the Master Budget

Once the functional budgets have been prepared and the necessary decisions taken about how the firm should respond to any limiting factors, the Master Budget can be prepared. The Master Budget is really a summary of the functional budgets and once prepared management will know the budgeted profit and loss for the coming period, together with the budgeted Balance Sheet showing the assets and liabilities of the business.

The Fisherman's Restaurant

Look at the figures for the Fisherman's Restaurant's sales and meals over their first six months' trading:

Sales	Jan	Feb	Mar	Apr	May	Jun
Meals	2,000	2,500	3,000	4,000	4,500	6,000
Direct labour hours worked	80	90	100	104	120	120

- Direct labour costs are £3.50 per hour. Other staff costs are £400 per month. All labour costs are paid in the month of production.

- The restaurant has leasing payments of £150 per month.

- The restaurant's rent is £16,000 per annum. The first quarterly payment is due in January.

- Food costs are £3 per meal and the restaurant receives 1 month's credit from suppliers.

- The business has just negotiated a £20,000 interest-only bank loan. The interest rate is 14% and it is payable quarterly. The first interest payment is due in March.

- All meals are sold for £9.

- In March, the restaurant has to purchase new kitchen equipment which will cost £3,000 and in May the firm will take delivery of a new carpet for £500. In June the restaurant will renew the 100-year lease on its premises for £80,000.

- The firm operates a "just in time" stock control system, and so it has no opening or closing stock.

- The restaurant currently has a cash balance of £23,000.

The restaurant's accountants have prepared a Cash Budget and Budgeted Profit and Loss Account and Balance Sheet for the business, shown in Figures 14.2–14.4.

Budgeted Cash Budget

Figure 14.2   The Fisherman's Restaurant: Budgeted Cash Budget January–June Year 1

Receipts	Jan £	Feb £	Mar £	Apr £	May £	Jun £
Cash sales	18,000	22,500	27,000	36,000	40,500	54,000
Payments						
Dir. labour	280	315	350	364	420	420
Staff wages	400	400	400	400	400	400
Leasing costs	150	150	150	150	150	150
Rent	4,000			4,000		
Food		6,000	7,500	9,000	12,000	13,500
Interest		700				700
Equipment			3,000			
Carpet					500	
Lease						80,000
Total						
Expenses	4,830	6,865	12,100	13,914	13,470	95,170

Figure 14.2 continued over

Figure 14.2 continued

Receipts	Jan £	Feb £	Mar £	Apr £	May £	Jun £
Balance						
Op. bal.	23,000	56,170	71,805	86,705	108,791	135,821
Loan	20,000					
Receipts	18,000	22,500	27,000	36,000	40,500	54,000
	61,000	78,670	98,805	122,705	149,291	189,821
Expenses	4,830	6,865	12,100	13,914	13,470	95,170
Cl. bal.	56,170	71,805	86,705	108,791	135,821	94,651

Budgeted Profit and Loss Account

Figure 14.3   The Fisherman's Restaurant: Budgeted Profit and Loss Account, January–June Year 1

	£	£
Sales		198,000
Less		
Food costs	66,000	
Direct labour	2,149	
		68,149
Gross profit		129,851
Less Expenses:		
Staff wages	2,400	
Leasing payments	900	
Interest payments	1,400	
Rent	8,000	
Total expenses		12,700
Net profit		117,151

Budgeted Balance Sheet

Figure 14.4   The Fisherman's Restaurant: Budgeted Balance Sheet

		£
Fixed Assets		
Leasehold premises		80,000
Equipment		3,000
Fixtures and fittings		500
		83,500
Current Assets		
Bank	94,651	
Less liabilities		
Bank loan	20,000	
Creditors	18,000	
	38,000	
Working capital		56,651
Net assets		114,151
Capital		
Capital		23,000
Profit		117,151
		114,151

Fixed and flexible budgets

One major limitation of the Master Budget which has just been prepared is that it takes no account of the level of trading activity. We saw in Chapter 12 that costs can be separated according to behaviour: fixed costs do not alter with changes in activity, whereas variable costs do. It is helpful for management decision making if the budgets can be prepared in such a way that they take this into consideration.

A fixed budget takes no account of any changes in activity, whereas a flexible budget shows how costs and revenues will change according to the level of activity.

Chef Master: a flexible budget

Chef Master manufacture a range of knives. The factory can produce
10,000 knives a month if it operates at 100% capacity. The costs at that
level of output are:

	£
Rent	5,000
Direct materials per unit	7
Leasing charges	590
Direct labour per unit	5
Variable overheads per unit	2
Interest on bank loan	200
Indirect wages	1,000

Before preparing the firm's flexible budget it is a good idea to separate
the different costs according to their **behaviour**. This is shown in Figure
14.5. Figure 14.5 shows the flexible budget drawn up from this cost data.

Figure 14.5   Chef Master: separation of costs according to behaviour

Cost	Fixed/Variable	
	(F)	**(V)**
Rent	F	
Direct materials		V
Leasing charges	F	
Direct labour		V
Variable overhead		V
Bank interest	F	
Indirect wages	F	

Note: The **fixed** costs will remain the same regardless of the level of
output

The **variable** costs will alter as a percentage of the maximum level of
output, which is 10,000 knives.

Figure 14.6   Chef Master: Flexible Budget

Output levels (%)	70 £	80 £	90 £	100 £
Rent	5,000	5,000	5,000	5,000
Direct materials	49,000	56,000	63,000	70,000
Leasing charges	590	590	590	590
Direct labour	35,000	40,000	45,000	50,000
Variable overheads	14,000	16,000	18,000	20,000
Bank interest	200	200	200	200
Indirect wages	1,000	1,000	1,000	1,000
Total cost	104,790	118,790	132,790	146,790

By preparing a flexible budget Chef Master knows how its costs **alter** with **activity**, and it is therefore a very useful tool for making output decisions.

Benefits of budgetary control

Limiting factors and economies of scale

One main benefit of a system of budgetary control is that it highlights the limiting factors outlined above so that they can be resolved before problems arise.

If the firm lacks the necessary operational capacity, then decisons must be taken about additional investment and the likely returns which it will yield.

On the other hand, if a theatre has more seats than are currently being demanded then the Marketing Department may be able to stimulate sales by altering one or all of the variables of the marketing mix such as the selling price, the way the theatre is promoted and how seats are distributed. Such changes can often bring about increased sales, allowing the business to enjoy the benefits of **economies of scale**. There will also be times when it is best to accept a limitation because it is only likely to be short term. By adopting a budgetary control approach, the business should be able to arrive at a decision which is good for the firm as a whole, rather than one which benefits only a **particular functional area**.

Organisational planning and staff motivation

Budgetary control has the added advantage of forcing managers to concentrate on the future, and is therefore beneficial and supportive to the organisational planning process. If the process is conducted effectively staff should become more motivated to achieving goals which they have **participated in setting**.

Budgets, strategic objectives and monitoring progress

Budgets are a useful accounting tool for translating **strategic objectives** into **reality**. By thinking how the firm's resources should be used the best methods can be deployed and waste eliminated. Budgets also give management a useful yardstick for measuring performance so that they can take **corrective action** if actual results deviate from planned. Budgetary control should also be thought of as an important monitoring technique, because without feedback management will not know if their objectives are being achieved **in time** to be able to take the **necessary action**.

Study tasks

1 Sarah and Kate would like to establish better financial control procedures in the Croeso Hotel. They have asked you to prepare a flow chart outlining a system of budgetary control for their business.

2 Sarah and Kate wish to involve all the staff of the Croeso Hotel in this new budgetary process, and have decided to explain the benefits of the system at next week's staff meeting. Prepare a list of points they can use in their talk to make a case for the control system.

3 In coordinating the food and beverage budget Sarah and Kate have noticed that a dinner dance has been planned for the first Saturday in each month. Discussions with the restaurant manager confirm that to cater for an estimated 120 covers per dinner dance is impossible because the restaurant can only take 80. The Head Chef has, however, pointed out that the kitchens, having recently increased their capacity, can now cater for 140 covers.

> **(a)** What types of limiting factor are illustrated in this problem?
> **(b)** Prepare a short report for Sarah and Kate outlining how these limiting factors could be overcome and resolved.

4 Sarah and Kate are meeting their bank manager Lynn Harvey next month. She has asked them to bring a Cash Budget showing planned receipts and payments for the next six months. Using the following figures, draw up the Cash Budget for the Croeso Hotel.

Sales	Jan £	Feb £	Mar £	Apr £	May £	Jun £
Restaurant	35,000	42,000	47,000	52,000	48,000	55,000
Bar	12,000	14,000	16,500	18,000	16,750	19,000
Rooms	40,000	47,000	55,000	65,000	78,000	85,000
Leisure Complex	500	1,200	1,400	2,000	2,300	2,400

(a) All takings in the bar and leisure complex are for cash. 60% of the accommodation and restaurant sales are for cash, with the balance being received the following month.
(b) The food and beverage costs amount to 50% of sales. These costs are paid for each month.
(c) The hotel has leasing payments of £700 a month.
(d) Fixed costs are £12,500 a month. 25% payable in the month in which they are incurred, the balance being paid one month later.
(e) The hotel must pay a £34,000 tax bill in April.
(f) Opening balance is £45,000.

5 Sarah and Kate would like to know what profit the Croeso Hotel would make if the level of restaurant and bar sales stated in Question 4 was achieved. Prepare a budgeted Profit and Loss Account in marginal cost format showing the contribution and fixed costs during the six-month period.

6 Sarah and Kate are wondering how hotel occupancy will affect profitability. The Croeso Hotel has 40 rooms in total. These are made up of:

	£ per night per room
16 single rooms	52.50
18 standard double rooms	80.00
4 luxury double rooms	90.00
2 suites	125.00

Calculate the budgeted sales revenue at 50%, 60%, 70%, 80%, 90% and 100% levels of occupancy (for one night).

15 Establishing a Standard Costing and Variance Analysis System

Why does a business need standard costing?

A system of standard costing establishes what the **cost should be** to produce a particular item or service before work begins. Whilst the system has its roots in manufacturing industry, it is often used in the service sector. In the catering industry, standard costing techniques can be applied to the preparation of meals, for example.

The purpose of establishing a system of standard costing is to achieve tight control of costs by highlighting any differences between **actual** and **standard** costs. The differences (or **variances**), once detected can be investigated by management and corrective action taken where necessary.

Whilst standard costing and variance analysis are two separate management accounting techniques they are interrelated. A system of standard costing is only effective if management analyse the **reason for the variance**.

Advantages of a standard costing system

Standard costing and budgetary control

A system of standard costing supports a firm's **budgetary control** process. If the firm only has a system of budgetary control differences will only become apparent at the **end** of each budget period. The main advantage of standard costing is that differences between the actual costs and standard costs can be detected **as they occur**.

Standard costing and financial control

Introducing a system of standard costing into a business is expensive. It is therefore important that it improves the **financial control** of operations. For example, stock control procedures will be simplified because all goods, whether they be raw materials, work in progress or finished stock, will be valued at the **standard cost figure**. The complexities of using the stock pricing methods of Last in First Out (LIFO) and First in First Out (FIFO) are eliminated as a result.

With the detailed information that a standard costing system provides there is the added advantage that **prices** can be more accurately set. By highlighting variances the system also allows **management by exception**. This means that management need only investigate those costs which show a **variance**, thereby allowing them to concentrate on the main problem areas of the business.

Establishing standards

Direct and indirect costs

Standard costs can be set for the firm's direct and indirect costs. The **direct** costs of producing a meal will be the price of the food and the amount of ingredients used, together with the cost of paying the chef. In addition there will be the **indirect** costs, which can be divided into fixed and variable overheads, these will include the rent for the restaurant and the electricity bill.

Relevant cost information: standard cost cards

Before a system of standard costing can be implemented a range of information must be collected from different sections of the business. Material prices will be held by the Purchasing Department, wage rates by Personnel and overhead expenses by the Accounting Department. When all the necessary data has been collected together **standard cost cards** can be produced. These will **establish** and **itemise** the individual cost components of direct materials, labour and overheads. It should, however, be noted that in undertaking the calculation of standard costs consideration must be given to the effect of changes in the firm's **product mix** or improvements in **productivity**.

Direct materials

The price standard determined for materials such as food and beverages is based on prices obtained, negotiated and agreed with suppliers. The figure may take account of any future short-term price increases. If this is the case, the final standard will be based on the **average price** which the firm expects to pay during the life of the standard.

The price standard must also take into consideration **losses** which may occur due to pilferage, deterioration and wastage during the preparation process. In the hospitality industry food and beverages are valuable commodities and without a safe storage and stock control system they can soon be lost or stolen. Training is also important in preventing the wastage of expensive ingredients. Finally the standard must take account of the **quality** of the ingredients or raw materials to be used, and the **quantities** required.

Direct wages

Most businesses set their wage costs after they have carried out negotiations with the relevant trade unions. With the introduction of two-year agreements this part of the standard-setting process has been made easier because the labour rate is already known. In the hospitality, leisure and tourism industries very few employees belong to a trade union and as a result it can be quite difficult to plan future wage costs.

Calculating the time needed to carry out a task depends on the skill and experience of the staff, together with their degree of motivation. In determining the direct wage costs allowances must also be made for the time it takes to prepare equipment for use or to learn new processes or systems.

Conversion overhead

A firm will have information about the **historical cost** of its overheads. By using a standard costing system the aim is to set a standard for the overhead, and this is referred to as the "conversion overhead". Management can if they wish split the conversion overhead into its fixed and variable elements, but unless there are specific reasons for splitting the overheads into their fixed and variable elements it is best to treat them as being fixed. This is why most firms use only fixed overhead controls, calculated as follows:

$$\frac{\text{Conversion overhead cost}}{\text{Produced hours (or other suitable method)}} = \text{Standard overhead rate}$$

Revising standards

A firm should revise its standards whenever there are permanent changes in working methods or materials used. Alterations will also be needed if the variances from standards are so great as to make the standard meaningless. It is costly to change standards, and ideally any revisions will take place when the business prepares its annual Budget. If the firm values its stock at standard cost then any changes in standard will mean that all items held in stock must be **revalued**.

Variance analysis

Variance analysis is a process which identifies any differences between standard costs and actual costs. If the variance is adverse it means that the costs are more than the standard envisaged. An adverse variance is shown in brackets as the case studies later in this chapter show. If the variance is **favourable** it means that the costs are in fact less than the standard. Whether a variance is adverse or favourable, management should investigate the underlying reasons for the difference and where necessary take corrective action.

Variances can occur in the materials used to make a particular product. A sandwich bar could find that the amount of cheese and ham used in crusty rolls is more than was anticipated, for example. Likewise the number of staff employed in the sandwich bar and the fixed and variable overheads incurred in running the business may also differ from the standard: the rent may alter, or the gas bill could be larger than expected.

It is important that managers understand how to calculate variances, and can identify their causes. Once this has been undertaken management must decide what steps should be taken about the variances revealed.

Direct materials price variance ✳

This is defined as "the difference between the standard price and the actual purchase price for the actual quantity of the material". The variance can be calculated either at the **delivery** time or at the time of **usage**. The variance should be calculated as follows:

Actual quantity purchased × [Standard price − Actual price]

We will now examine how The Pancake Parlour deals with its variance problems on direct materials.

The Pancake Parlour: cost of Jam

Eg if needed

The Pancake Parlour has a standard cost of 50p per kg of strawberry jam and a standard usage of 200 kg. Rebecca Dawson, the restaurant's supervisor, has ordered 240 kg at 60p per kg, so we can calculate the direct material price variance:

> 240 × [50p – 60p]
>
> = 240 × (10p)
>
> = (£24) **Adverse**

Having identified that The Pancake Parlour paid £24 more for the jam than it had planned, the next stage is for management to find out **why this has happened**. There are a number of possible reasons:

- The supplier increased the price of the jam after the standard price had been set
- Prices have risen due to inflation
- The Pancake Parlour has not been able to place a large enough order to gain a trade discount
- A different supplier has been used.

Whatever the reason for the variance, management need to ensure the situation does not arise again. This could involve changing suppliers or renegotiating contracts.

Direct materials usage variance ✶

This is defined as "the difference between the standard quantity specified for the actual production, and the actual quantity used, at standard purchase price". The variance should be calculated as follows:

> [Standard quantity specified for actual production – Actual quantity used] × Standard price

The Pancake Parlour; usage of Jam   eg if needed

Rebecca Dawson ordered 240 kg instead of the 200 kg as set in the standard. Using our formula, the material usage variance is:

$$(200 - 240) \times 50p$$
$$= [40] \times 50p$$
$$= (£20) \textbf{ Adverse}$$

From this calculation it can be seen that too much jam has been used. This could be due, for example, to:

- Wastage or carelessness in storage
- Poor quality jam.

Direct labour variance

This is "the difference between the standard and the actual direct labour cost incurred for the production achieved". The variance is calculated as follows:

(Standard direct labour hours produced × Standard rate per hour)

Less

(Actual direct labour hours worked × Actual rate per hour)

We will use the example of a conference organiser to show how labour variances can be controlled.

Class One: set-up times

Class One a firm of conference and event organisers, established a standard labour cost for setting up a travel exhibition in Edinburgh. The company set a standard time of forty hours at £5 per hour. The number of hours actually required to set up the exhibition stands was 54 hours. The direct labour variance is therefore:

```
            £
40 × £5 = 200      Standard cost
54 × £5 = 270      Actual cost
          (£70)    Adverse
```

This shows that the company took 14 hours longer to set up the exhibition, and so management need to find out the reason for the extra time. It could be due to:

- Delays in the arrival of the exhibition stands
- Lack of staff training in how to put up new equipment
- Changes to meet the wishes of the organisers.

Direct labour rate variance ✴

This is defined as "the difference between the standard and the actual direct labour hourly rate taking into account the total hours worked or paid". The variance is calculated as follows:

(Standard rate per hour − Actual rate per hour)
Multiplied by the Actual hours worked or paid

Class One: set-up costs

Assuming that Class One had to pay £6.00 per hour for the 54 hours of labour employed to set up the travel exhibition then the direct labour rate variance would be:

£5 − £6 × 54 hours

= £1 × 54

= (£54) **Adverse**

This could be due to a new pay rise which has increased hourly labour rates.

Direct labour efficiency variance ✳

This is "the difference between the standard hours for the actual production achieved and the hours actually worked, valued at the standard labour rate". It is calculated as follows:

> (Standard hours produced – Actual hours worked) × Standard rate per hour

Class One: set-up efficiency

Class One set a standard of 40 hours at a rate of £5 per hour. The work was completed in 54 hours at a labour cost of £6 per hour. The direct labour efficiency was therefore:

> $(40 - 54) \times £5$
>
> $= (-14) \times £5$
>
> $= (£70)$ **Adverse**

This highlights the extra incurred because the task could not be completed on time.

Overhead variances

Standards can be set for both **fixed** and **variable** overheads. The former will usually be time-related and the latter activity-related. An overhead variance is defined as "the difference between budgeted and actual overhead expenditure". Fixed overhead variances are calculated as follows:

> Fixed overhead budgeted cost – Actual conversion overhead incurred

Variable overhead variance is calculated as follows:

> (Actual units produced × Variable overhead absorption rate per unit) less Actual cost

We will use the budget from Chill Fresh Foods to explore their problems with fixed and variable overheads.

Chill Fresh Foods: overhead expenditure

Chill Fresh Foods has produced the following budget for its cook chill snack meals operation:

> **Budgeted fixed overhead** = £144,000 per annum over a 48-week year
> = £3,000 per week
> **Budgeted production** = 48,000 units per annum over 48-week year
> = 1,000 units per week
>
> **Variable overhead** for the year is expected to be £24,000
> **Actual output** for the week under review
> 1,010 units and the **actual fixed overhead cost** was £3,100
> **Actual variable overhead expenditure** was £625

It is best to calculate the **variable overhead expense variance** first:

$$\frac{\text{Budgeted cost}}{\text{Units of output}} = \frac{£24,000}{48,000} = £0.50 \text{ per unit (meal)}$$

Once the unit variable overhead cost has been calculated the **fixed overhead expenditure variance** can be worked out.

> Budgeted fixed conversion overhead − Actual fixed conversion overhead incurred.
> 3,000 − 3,100 = (£100) **Adverse**

The **variable overhead variance** is calculated as follows:

> (Actual units produced × Variable overhead absorption rate) − Actual cost
>
> (1,010 × 0.50) − 625 = (£120) **Adverse**

Chill Fresh Foods therefore found there were 10 more units produced, which cost the firm an extra £5 on variable overheads.

Standard cost comparison statement

The real value of calculating these variances comes from comparing **actual** performance with **budgeted**. By summarising all of the variances management can see what action will have to be taken to make actual performance the same as the standard set. How this can be presented can be seen from the figures produced by Saddles and Reins for the first quarter of their operations.

Saddles and Reins: output and standard costs

Saddles and Reins make a range of equipment for equestrians. The company use a standard costing system and the first half year output level, together with the standard costs, are shown in Figure 15.1.

Figure 15.1   Saddles and Reins: first half year figures

	Budgeted Output £	Standard Cost £	Actual Cost £
Sales	30,000	20	260,000
Materials		6	97,000
Labour		4	54,000
Factory variable overheads		2	30,000
Factory fixed overheads		2	28,000

Profit and Loss Account	Budgeted £	Actual £
Sales	300,000	260,000

Profit and Loss Account	**Budgeted** £	**Actual** £
Less		
Materials	90,000	97,000
Labour	60,000	54,000
Variable overheads	30,000	30,000
Fixed overheads	30,000	28,000
	210,000	209,000
Profit	90,000	51,000
Budgeted profit		90,000
Sales variance (**Adverse**)	(40,000)	
Materials variance (**Adverse**)	(7,000)	
Labour variance **Favourable**	6,000	
Fixed overheads		
variance **Favourable**	2,000	
		(39,000)
Actual profit		51,000

Normal and ideal standards

If a firm is to benefit from a standard costing system it must introduce it carefully, explaining fully the benefits and involving staff in the setting of standards: if the standards are seen as punitive or unfair it is unlikely that the system will benefit the firm. A firm can base its system on either a **normal** or an **ideal standard**. The normal standard takes into account normal wastage and operator failure and is therefore more appropriate for businesses in the hospitality and leisure industries. The ideal standard makes no allowance for wastage or human error and is best suited for process industries where production processes are controlled by computer.

Study tasks

1   Sarah and Kate are now considering introducing a standard costing system to the rest of the hotel. What benefits should the Croeso Hotel receive from using such a system, and how should the standards be set?

2   The Croeso Hotel has recently installed a standard costing system in its food and beverage department. Sarah and Kate are comparing actual costs with standard costs in the kitchen:

> • The hotel has set a standard cost of 45p per kg of flour and a standard usage of 1,500 kg per week. Monica Petrocelli, the part-time pastry chef has used 1,800 kg. at 50p per kg Calculate the direct ingredient usage variance.
>
> • The standard cost of cream is 64p and the standard usage 500 pints per month. Monica has used 425 pints. Calculate the direct ingredient usage variance.

3   Sarah and Kate have also been comparing actual and standard cleaning costs:

> • The hotel has a standard of 4 hours' cleaning after a conference at a cost of £3.50 per hour. The cleaners took 3 hours. Calculate the direct labour variance.
>
> • The hotel has a standard time of cleaning the beer cellar in one hour at £6 an hour. The work was completed in 1½ hours at a cost of £4 per hour. Calculate the direct labour variance.

4   Sarah and Kate then looked at actual and standard costs in the restaurant and bar:

> • The Valley View bar has set a standard cost of 60p per bottle of orange juice and a standard usage of 2,000 bottles a month. The Head bar person George Wilson has ordered 2,400 bottles at 66p per bottle. Calculate the direct material price variance.
>
> • The Victoria Restaurant has set a standard of 64p per pint of organic milk and a standard usage of 500 pints per month. Hugh Roberts has used 425 pints at 62p a pint. Calculate the direct material price variance.

5 The Croeso Hotel has operated a standard costing system for the first quarter of its current financial year. Prepare the hotel's costing Trading and Profit and Loss Account and compare the budgeted with the actual profit for the first quarter.

	Budgeted Output	Standard £	Actual £
Sales	15,000	22.50	13,500
Food		12.00	102,000
Labour		6.00	61,500
Hotel Overheads		3.00	24,000

6 Catherine Jenkins manages the front office department and has carried out an analysis of the costs incurred. She is pleased that the variance is favourable and has concluded that there is no need to mention this in her monthly report. Why may her costs have shown a favourable variance, and is Catherine correct in thinking that there is no need to draw Sarah and Kate's attention to it?

Part III
Financial Analysis

16 Interpreting Financial Accounts

Understanding financial performance

Company accounts are always audited so that they can be filed at Companies House and submitted to the Inland Revenue. Although these documents show the assets, liabilities, revenue and expenditure, together with the profit or loss which a business has made each year, the owners, managers and other interested parties usually like to know more about their company's financial performance. In order to gain this deeper understanding they need to learn how to carry out **ratio analysis**.

What is an accounting ratio?

An accounting ratio, like an arithmetic ratio, is useful when analysing two sets of numbers. A ratio is not concerned with the precise measurement of numbers but rather the **relationship** between two or more sets of figures.

If a business person invests £100,000 in assets and has a bank loan of £20,000 the ratio of borrowed funds to assets can be shown in a variety of different ways. It could be said that:

(a) The ratio of assets to borrowings is **5:1**
(b) The ratio of borrowing to assets is **1:5**
(c) Assets represent five times (**5 ×**) liabilities
(d) Loans represent **1/5** of assets
(e) Loans represent **20%** of assets.

There is no agreed procedure amongst accountants about how company information should be compared, but convention has dictated that some information is presented as a ratio while other information is shown as a percentage. In either case, however, the term "accounting ratio" is used.

Ratio analysis and financial performance

In order to determine how **effectively** a business is being managed, information is needed about how it **uses** its **assets** to **generate profits**. Ratio analysis is a useful management tool for examining trends in a firm's financial performance. It is the **trend** which is important, because one needs to gain an understanding of the financial performance of the business **over a period of time**. Comparisons can then be made with the previous year's financial performance, and how it relates to other similar companies operating in the same industry.

Using accounting ratios

There are many accounting ratios which seek to appraise the financial strengths and weaknesses of any business. They can, however, be categorised into **five** key groups. If the analysis is to be a thorough review of the firm's operations it needs to monitor and assess:

> - Liquidity
> - Profitability
> - Use of assets
> - Capital structure
> - Returns paid to investors.

The first step is to **isolate** the relevant figures shown in the accounts and then to use them to **calculate** the ratios. Once this has been completed, the figures need to be **interpreted** and **explained**.

The rest of this chapter will now show you how to calculate the necessary ratios as well as providing an explanation of what the ratio reveals.

Sports Wise: trading accounts

Jeff Rogers and Chandra Patel met when they were both at college following a Business Studies course which included the option to study some leisure and tourism units. Chandra was keen to set up his own business when he finished the course and he asked Jeff to become the manager of the sports equipment shop he was opening with his two brothers.

Sports Wise has been operating for two years and Chandra has asked Jeff to prepare a report on the financial performance of the business. The Profit and Loss Accounts and Balance Sheets for the first two years of trading are produced in Figure 16.1; we will then look at the details of the ratio calculations Jeff has carried out.

Figure 16.1   Sports Wise: Profit and Loss Accounts for years ended 5 April 1 and 2 Year

	Year 1 £	Year 2 £
Sales	400,000	500,000
Less cost of sales	125,000	170,000
Gross profit	275,000	330,000
Less Expenses		
Wages	50,000	74,000
Rates	29,000	32,000
Interest payment	26,000	36,000
Overheads	30,000	58,000
Net profit before tax	140,000	130,000

Balance Sheets as at 5 April	Year 1 £	Year 2 £
Fixed Assets: at cost less depreciation		
Shop premises	500,000	500,000
Fixtures and fittings	260,000	287,500
Motor vehicles	30,000	30,000
Current Assets		
Stock	140,000	275,000
Debtors	180,000	200,000
Bank and Cash	310,000	225,000

Figure continued over

Less Current Liabilities

Creditors	15,000	40,000
Tax	80,000	70,000
Bank overdraft	615,000	660,000
Net Assets	710,000	747,500

Financed by

Share Capital ord. shares £1 fully paid	450,000	450,000
Reserves	–	37,500
Mortgage	260,000	260,000
Capital employed	710,000	747,500

Notes to the accounts

		Year 1	Year 2
(1)	Opening stocks	180,000	140,000
	Purchases	85,000	305,000
		265,000	445,000
	Less closing stocks	140,000	275,000
	Cost of sales	125,000	170,000
(2)	Profit before tax	140,000	130,000
	Less taxation	80,000	70,000
		60,000	60,000
	Less Dividend	15,000	22,500
	Retained profit	45,000	37,500

Liquidity

"Liquidity" is the word accountants use to describe **how much cash a business has**. Expenses can only be settled with cash, and so these ratios seek to measure the **solvency** of the firm. There are two main ratios – current ratio and acid test ratios.

Current ratio

The **current ratio or working capital ratio** is calculated by dividing the current assets by the current liabilities. Current assets are the short-term trading assets which are needed for everyday operations. On the Balance Sheet, they are always shown in order of liquidity so that the most illiquid asset is listed first and the most liquid last. The order is:

- Stock
- Debtors
- Bank
- Cash balances.

The amount of **stock** which must be held will be influenced by the level of sales and the management's ability to control stock levels. Similarly, the amount of money invested in **debtors** will be dependent on the level of credit sales and the organisation's ability to operate an efficient and effective credit control policy.

The **current liabilities** show the amount of money owed short term and which must be repaid within 1 year of the Balance Sheet date.

Any business should have more money invested in current assets than current liabilities, and for many establishments a ratio of **2:1** is considered a sensible ratio. The exact ratio will again depend on the type of industry in which the firm is engaged but will be influenced by the speed at which it can convert its stock into cash. The quicker this can be achieved the less money is tied up in stock, and as a result the firm will be more profitable and able to operate on a lower ratio. The current ratio is calculated as follows:

$$\frac{\text{Current assets}}{\text{Current liabilities}}$$

Sports Wise: current ratios

The current ratios for Sports Wise are shown in Figure 16.2.

Figure 16.2   Sports Wise: the liquidity problem

Extracts	Year 1 £	Year 2 £
Current Assets		
Stock	140,000	275,000
Debtors	180,000	200,000
Bank and cash	310,000	225,000
	630,000	700,000
Current Liabilities		
Creditors	15,000	40,000
Tax	80,000	70,000
Bank overdraft	615,000	660,000
	710,000	770,000

$$\textbf{Year 1} \qquad \frac{630,000}{710,000} = 0.89:1$$

$$\textbf{Year 2} \qquad \frac{700,000}{770,000} = 0.91:1$$

These two ratios indicate that Sports Wise has a liquidity problem, although in Year 2 the figures reveal a slight improvement on Year 1. Jeff needs to look at the **stock and debtors** totals carefully, and decide what action needs to be taken:

- **Stock levels** could be reduced

- **Debtors** could be too high – policies need to be developed to decrease this figure

Jeff also needs to study the **current liabilities**, and decide what steps can be taken to improve the situation:

- Creditors could be reduced by ensuring that **over-ordering** does not take place, leading to high levels of stock
- The **bank overdrafts** should be reduced where possible by limiting the credit given to debtors.

Acid test ratio

Whilst the current ratio is important as a measure of solvency, it does not show the liquid resources which are available to meet the **short-term liabilities**. Current liabilities can only be paid in cash and so the **Acid test ratio** (sometimes referred to as the Quick ratio) is used. This is calculated by taking the current assets total, minus the stock figures, and dividing by the current liabilities figure.

The minimum ratio here should be 1:1, but once again it will depend upon the level of **stock turnover** and the speed with which current assets can be converted into cash. Fast food chains are able to operate below this ratio and are therefore able to use creditors' money to finance part of their day-to-day business expenses. This helps them achieve high profit ratios but if other businesses in the hospitality industry tried the same strategy they would soon find themselves insolvent because of their inability to turn stock into cash in such a short time. The ratio is calculated as follows:

$$\frac{\text{Current assets} - \text{Stock}}{\text{Current liabilities}}$$

Sports Wise: acid test ratios

The final accounts for Sports Wise for Year 1 and Year 2 reveal the acid test ratios shown in Figure 16.2.

Figure 16.2   Sports Wise: declining liquidity in Year 2

Extracts	Year 1 £	Year 2 £
Current Assets		
Debtors	180,000	200,000
Bank and Cash	310,000	225,000
	490,000	425,000
Current Liabilities		
Creditors	15,000	40,000
Tax	80,000	70,000
Bank overdraft	615,000	660,000
	710,000	770,000

$$\text{Year 1} \quad \frac{490,000}{710,000} = 0.69:1$$

$$\text{Year 2} \quad \frac{425,000}{770,000} = 0.55:1$$

The ratio for Year 2 shows a decline in liquidity, and a strategy is needed for improving Sports Wise acid test ratio. In essence, this means finding ways of reducing the **current liabilities** amount.

Profitability

Profitability ratios show the **percentage profit** which is being earned by the business, both before and after it has paid its expenses. These two ratios are **Gross profit/Sales** and **Net profit/Sales**. Both are calculated using information in the Profit and Loss Account.

Gross profit/sales ratio

The gross profit/sales ratio illustrates what margin the firm is able to make on each sale. The ratio is calculated as follows:

$$\frac{\text{Gross profit}}{\text{Sales}} \times 100$$

As a general rule if the business enjoys large sales a smaller gross profit per sale will be sufficient to provide an adequate gross profit.

Sports Wise: decreasing gross profit margin

By looking at Sports Wise's Profit and Loss Accounts for Year 1 and Year 2 the gross profit/sales ratio can be calculated (see Figure 16.4).

Figure 16.4   Sports Wise: profits and sales, Year 1 and 2

Extracts	**Year 1** **£**	**Year 2** **£**
Sales	400,000	500,000
Less Cost of sales	125,000	170,000
Gross profit	275,000	330,000

Year 1 $\dfrac{275,000 \times 100}{400,000} = 69\%$

Year 2 $\dfrac{330,000 \times 100}{500,000} = 66\%$

These profits and sales figures demonstrate that Sports Wise's gross profit margin has decreased by 3% between 1 and 2 Years. In other words, the **cost of sales** has increased by 3% during the period in question. As the manager of the shop, Jeff will need to research why this increase in cost of sales has occurred, and attempt to remedy the problem(s). It is likely that the increase is due to a combination of factors:

- Increased cost of purchases due to **supplier's price** rises
- Changes in **customer requirements**, leading to a demand for less expensive equipment
- Price competition leading to reduced profit margins

Net profit/sales ratio

Once the gross margin has been calculated it is useful to know how much **profit** is used to pay the expenses incurred in operating the business. The higher they are, the more profit which must be earned just to cover the businesses' costs. Once again, this ratio is expressed as a percentage and is calculated as follows:

$$\frac{\text{Net Profit}}{\text{Sales}} \times 100$$

It is difficult to say exactly what percentage profit should be earned from each sale, as this will depend on the costs of each business and will therefore vary from industry to industry. Whatever percentage profit is being earned it must be sufficient to pay all expenses, provide an adequate return to the owners and leave sufficient profit within the business to finance new investment which will generate profits in future years.

Sports Wise: decreasing net profit/sales ratio

We can calculate the net profit/sales ratios for Sports Wise as in Figure 16.5.

Figure 16.5   Sports Wise: expenses/costs increase

Extracts	Year 1 £	Year 2 £
Gross profit	275,000	330,000
Less Expenses		
Wages	50,000	74,000
Rates	29,000	32,000
Interest payments	26,000	36,000
Overheads	30,000	58,000
Net profit before tax	140,000	130,000

Year 1 $\dfrac{140,000}{400,000} \times 100 = 35\%$

Year 2 $\dfrac{130,000}{500,000} \times 100 = 26\%$

As can be seen, Sports Wise's net profit/sales has decreased by 9% during the two-year period. While the business has made a larger gross profit the **expenses** of the business have also increased. The owners need to know why these costs have increased, and consider ways of reducing them so that they only rise in line with future sales and profits. The increase in wage costs could have occurred because:

- **Wage rises** have been given to staff
- **More staff** have been recruited
- Of increases in **employee benefits**
- A significant amount of **overtime** worked.

Strategy for cost reduction

Some of these cost increases are within Jeff's control, whilst some are not:

- The increase in **business rates** is beyond Sports Wise's control, as rates are set by the local council.

- **Interest rates** vary according to the state of the general economy. Sports Wise's increase suggests either that the interest rate has risen over the past year or that the company's debt level has itself been increased. The Balance Sheet reveals that the latter has occurred. Chandra and his brothers can only remedy this situation by reducing their overdraft:

    ★ **Increasing profits** and repaying part of the loan
    ★ **Selling surplus assets** to repay part of the debt.

- **Overheads** include all those other expenses incurred in running a business – for example, electricity, gas, stationery, advertising. Jeff needs to review each item of expenditure and develop practical solutions to control these costs:

    ★ An **energy saving** campaign
    ★ Stock control procedures for **office stationery.**

- When sales are increased managers and investors hope that **profit** will also increase. In Sports Wise's case, they have fallen, which suggests that either the firm is unable to pass on all of its costs to customers or that it is gaining sales at the expense of profit.

Use of assets

Businesses place investors' money in assets which are used to earn profits. The greater the return which can be derived from the assets, the more attractive the investment, and the more profitable the firm. There are a number of ratios which aim to measure how effectively any business uses its assets:

- Sales/fixed assets
- Stock turnover
- Collection time of debtors
- Time taken to pay creditors
- Fixed/current assets.

Ratio of sales to fixed assets

Fixed assets are required so that the firm can carry on its main business activity. In theory, the greater the investment in fixed assets, the greater the level of sales. Ideally, the level of **sales** should be greater than the investment in **fixed assets**, thereby showing that each £ invested in fixed assets can generate extra sales income. The ratio is calculated as follows:

$$\frac{\text{Sales}}{\text{Fixed assets}}$$

Sports Wise: improving sales/fixed assets ratio

Look at Figure 16.6.

Figure 16.6   Sports Wise: sales generated by fixed assets

Extract	Year 1 £	Year 2 £
Sales	400,000	500,000
Fixed Assets		
Shop premises	500,000	500,000
Fixtures and fittings	260,000	287,500
Motor vehicles	30,000	30,000
	790,000	817,500

In **Year 1** the ratio for the shop was:

$$\frac{400,000}{790,000} = 0.51:1$$

In **Year 2** the ratio for the shop was:

$$\frac{500,000}{817,500} = 0.61:1$$

The ratios for Year 1 and Year 2 indicate that the fixed assets are not generating sufficient sales. However, the ratio by Year 2 shows an improvement on the Year 1 figure: the owners must consider ways of **increasing business turnover**.

The stock turnover ratio

This ratio measures how many times the firm can sell its entire stock during a year. The **quicker** stock can be sold, the more profitable the firm and the less money needed to be invested in stock. Generally speaking, if the business enjoys a high stock turnover rate then it makes a small margin each time it sells its stock, whereas if the stock turnover rate is low, it must make a higher profit when it sells its stock.

The stock turnover ratio is calculated as follows:

$$\frac{\text{Average stock}}{\text{Cost of Sales}} \times \frac{365}{1}$$

(the average stock is calculated by adding together the opening and closing figures for the year and dividing by two).

Sports Wise: improving stock turnover

Look at Figure 16.7.

Figure 16.7   Sports Wise: stock turnover figures

Extracts	Year 1 £	Year 2 £
Average stock	$\dfrac{180{,}000 + 140{,}000}{2}$	$\dfrac{140{,}000 + 275{,}000}{2}$
Stock turnover	$\dfrac{160{,}00 \times 365}{125{,}000}$	$\dfrac{207{,}500 \times 365}{170{,}000}$
	= 467 days	= 446 days

The quicker a firm can sell its stock, the **less liquid** it needs to be, because it has reduced the time and stockholding costs.

Sports Wise's stock turnover figure indicates that the rate of stock turnover is low, although it is getting marginally better. This will inevitably lead to liquidity problems and is likely to result in the firm taking longer to pay its creditors.

Collection time of debtors

Many sales are made **on credit**. When this happens the firm selling the goods is effectively financing the other business, and so the quicker it can be paid the quicker the money can be invested in more current assets which will earn additional profit. By using the ratio

$$\frac{\text{Debtors}}{\text{Sales}} \times 365$$

one can see how long it takes the firm to be paid.

Sports Wise: inefficient credit control

Look at Figure 16.8.

Figure 16.8   Sports Wise: collection of debtors' figures

Extracts	Year 1 £	Year 2 £
Sales	400,000	500,000
Debtors	180,000	200,000

In **Year 1** the ratio was: $\dfrac{180,000}{400,000} \times \dfrac{365}{1} = 164$ days

In **Year 2** the ratio was: $\dfrac{200,000}{500,000} \times \dfrac{365}{1} = 146$ days

It can be seen that Sports Wise is allowing too long for debtors to pay their accounts. Jeff needs to develop an efficient credit control policy to rectify the situation:

- Offering customers **cash discount** for prompt payment
- Sending **reminder letters** to outstanding account holders.

Debtors should be kept to a minimum and collection of the payment should be vigorously enforced – some firms threaten legal action if payment is not forthcoming. Firms often find it necessary, in order to obtain or secure contracts, to offer credit terms which are as good or better than those of their competitors, and such large credit sales can put considerable strain on working capital.

Time taken to pay creditors

If the firm can receive cash from its debtors before having to meet its creditors, it is effectively receiving **interest-free** credit and so it is able to use other firms' money to finance its day-to-day trading.

The ratio is calculated as follows:

$$\frac{\text{Trade creditors}}{\text{Purchases}} \times \frac{365}{1}$$

Sports Wise: slow payment of creditors

Look at Figure 16.9.

Figure 16.9   Sports Wise: payment of creditors' figures

Extracts	Year 1 £	Year 2 £
Creditors	15,000	40,000
Notes to the Accounts		
Purchases	85,000	305,000

In Year 1 the ratio was: $\dfrac{15,000}{85,000} \times \dfrac{365}{1} = $ 64 days

In Year 2 the ratio was: $\dfrac{40,000}{305,000} \times \dfrac{365}{1} = $ 48 days

Sports Wise's two ratios show that the firm is receiving less credit and this is adding to its liquidity problems.

Fixed assets to current assets

Fxed assets are needed to operate a business, but generally it is the **current assets** which earn the profits for the firm. The higher the ratio of current assets to fixed assets, the more profitable the firm should be. If a business has too high a percentage of its capital invested in fixed assets it should consider selling some, thereby increasing its ratio of fixed to current assets. The ratio is calculated as follows:

$$\frac{\text{Fixed assets}}{\text{Current assets}}$$

Sports Wise: increase in income-generating assets

Look at Figure 16.10.

Figure 16.10   Sports Wise: current and fixed assets

Extracts	Year 1	Year 2
	£	£
Fixed Assets		
Shop premises	500,000	500,000
Fixtures and fittings	260,000	287,500
Motor vehicles	30,000	30,000
	790,000	817,500
Current Assets		
Stock	140,000	275,000
Debtors	180,000	200,000
Bank and cash	310,000	225,000
	630,000	700,000

In **Year 1** the ratio was: $\dfrac{790,000}{630,000} = 1.25:1$

In **Year 2** the ratio was: $\dfrac{817,500}{700,000} - 1.17:1$

Figure 16.10 demonstrates a slight decrease in the ratio which shows that Sports Wise is increasing the ratio of its income-generating assets to its fixed assets.

Capital structure

Capital structure ratios show how the firm is **financed**, and what the firm can **earn** with the capital invested in the business.

Gearing ratio

The gearing ratio seeks to measure the **level of debt to equity capital**. A business can finance itself in two ways. Firstly the owners can invest their savings in the business, and secondly they can borrow additional funds from outside sources. The ratio measures the level of

$$\frac{\text{Debt}}{\text{Equity}}$$

debt to equity capital. The higher the debt capital, the greater the risk for there is always a danger that the business may be unable to meet its **interest costs** if its sales and profits fall. For this reason, investors generally prefer to see most of the money being provided by the owners.

Sports Wise: financing by short-term sources

Look at Figure 16.11.

Figure 16.11   Sports Wise: short-term capital figures

Extract	Year 1 £	Year 2 £
Mortgage	260,000	260,000
Share capital	450,000	450,000
Reserves	–	37,500
	450,000	487,500

In **Year 1** the gearing ratio was: $\dfrac{260,000}{450,000} = 0.58:1$

In **Year 2** the gearing ratio was: $\dfrac{260,000}{450,000} = 0.58:1$

Debt capital

The main problem in using the gearing ratio is to determine what should be included in **debt capital**. Some analysts include all borrowing, so creditors and bank overdrafts are considered to be part of the firm's debt capital. This is taking a very strict view. Other, more lenient, analysts only include long-term debt, that is debt capital which does not have to be repaid within 1 year from the Balance Sheet date.

If the business can raise debt capital cheaper than equity, it makes sense to borrow the money. By doing this, the firm will be able to reduce its overall cost of capital. If too much debt is raised, however, both shareholders and lenders will require higher returns because of the perceived increased risks: this will inevitably increase the firm's cost of capital.

The gearing ratio is important because if a firm increases its debt capital unduly, it may not be able to meet all of its interest charges from its profits, and as a result may be wound up by its creditors.

During Year 2, Sports Wise has not increased its long-term debt but its short-loan debt has increased dramatically. Most worrying is the increase in creditors and bank overdraft. Technically its overdraft is repayable on demand, and so the business is financing too much of its capital from short-term sources.

Returns paid to investors

Return on capital employed (ROCE)

All firms use the capital invested in their business to **earn a return** for the owners (shareholders). The main problem is defining what the amount of "capital" is which is financing the firm. Many companies will have raised finance from shareholders and long-term lenders, and so the broadest definition will include all long-term capital when calculating the return from capital employed. A narrow definition only includes share capital and reserves, because this is the amount of money which the owners have invested in the business. Whenever one is comparing the return on capital employed of different businesses it is therefore important to know whether a **broad** or **narrow** definition of capital employed has been used.

The ratio is calculated as follows:

$$\frac{\text{Profit (before interest to debt holders)}}{\text{Capital employed}} \times 100$$

Sports Wise: increase in capital base

Look at Figure 16.12.

Figure 16.12   Sports Wise: ROCE figures

Extract	Year 1 £	Year 2 £
Profit before tax	140,000	130,000
Add Interest payments	26,000	36,000
	166,000	166,000
Capital Capital employed	710,000	747,500

$$\frac{166,000 \times 100}{710,000} = 23\% \qquad \frac{166,000 \times 100}{747,500} = 22\%$$

Sports Wise's return on capital employed has been calculated using the broader definition of capital, because both shareholders' funds and long-term debt capital have been included in the definition of capital. The return has fallen slightly even though the firm has made the same profit (before interest and tax) in each year, because the addition of £37,500 retained profit has increased the shareholders' capital base.

Whenever a business increases its capital base it will be able to employ additional assets and one would therefore expect an increase in the return which can be made from these assets. In the short term, major investments may result in a lower return on capital employed until they can generate the desired return.

Earnings per share

This ratio shows how much profit each share has earned during the current year. It is a useful ratio, for it shows the **return** which can be made by **investing in the business**. The higher its percentage, the greater the return. The ratio is calculated as follows:

$$\frac{\text{Profit after tax and preference share dividend}}{\text{No. of issued ordinary shares}}$$

Sports Wise: falling EPS

It is unusual for a company to distribute all of its profit as dividends to shareholders but the higher the earnings the more profit can be distributed. As a result, investors are always seeking companies which can earn high returns. Look at Figure 16.13.

Figure 16.13   Sports Wise: EPS figures

Extracts	Profit before tax plus interest payments	
Year 1	140,000 + 26,000	$\dfrac{166,000 \times 100}{710,000} = 23\%$
Year 2	130,000 + 36,000	$\dfrac{166,000 \times 100}{747,500} = 22\%$

Dividend yield

This ratio is calculated as follows:

$$\frac{\text{Ordinary dividend per share}}{\text{Market price per share}} \times \frac{100}{\pounds1}$$

Shares are usually bought at their **market value** rather than at their **nominal value**. The dividend yield shows what percentage of the market price the investor will receive as a dividend for payment. As Sports Wise is a private company, the ratio cannot be calculated. If, however, the shares had a market price of (say) £1.25 in Year 1 and £1.40 in Year 2, and a 5p dividend per share was possible for both years, the yield would be:

Year 1 $\dfrac{5 \times 100}{125p} = 4\%$ **Year 2** $\dfrac{5 \times 100}{140p} = 3.6\%$

Dividend cover

This ratio is calculated as follows:

$$\frac{\text{Profit after tax less preference share dividend}}{\text{Gross dividend on ordinary shares}}$$

This ratio illustrates how much more dividend could have been paid out of current earnings. A shareholder's "return" from an investment consists of dividends plus any capital gains in the share price. So if a company can reinvest its earning profitably, a shareholder may be content not to get a higher dividend in the current year.

Year 1 $\dfrac{60,000}{37,500} = 1.6{:}1$ **Year 2** $\dfrac{65,000}{37,500} = 1.7 : 1$

The higher the dividend cover ratio, the more money being reinvested in the business which should earn profits in the future and increase shareholder wealth.

Ratio analysis in action

Ratios are a useful technique for analysing the accounts of firms. It is important to realise, however, that they are not a substitute for sound financial performance, and that they do have their limitations. The following **seven** points should always be kept in mind when using ratio analysis:

- Ratios are only as "sound" as the information on which they are **based**

- Ratios can only **indicate future trends**, they cannot guarantee them

- When interpreting trends, the **general economic climate** has to be taken into account

- Trends may differ due to alterations in **accounting methods** from one period to the next, and between firms

- It is not always easy to make straightforward comparisons with **other companies**

- Accounting figures are not always precise – there may be an element of individual **judgement** in them

- Other vital information about the firm may be disregarded because it is not expressed in **financial terms**.

Study tasks

1 Sarah and Kate have been to the local reference library and obtained the following data about companies trading in the hospitality industry. They would like you to interpret the following ratios and explain their implications for them:

Ratio	Upper quartile	Median	Lower quartile
Current ratio	2:1	1.5:1	0.7:1
Acid test	1.2:1	1:1	0.8:1
Stock turnover	12	8	6
Sales to debtors	53 days	35 days	25 days
Return on capital employed	27%	20%	15%
Earnings per share	22p	18p	15p
Dividend yield	9p	7p	4p
Gearing	1:1	0.5:1	0.3:1

2 Sarah and Kate have just had a visit from Ralph Simons, their accountant. He has informed them that their business may have a liquidity problem if they do not take some urgent action. The two women are not quite sure what Ralph means, and they have asked you to prepare a brief report outlining:

> **(a)** What is meant by the term "liquidity"?
> **(b)** How is liquidity measured?
> **(c)** What action should they take to overcome any potential liquidity problems?

3 Stephen and Jill Conway are two of Kate's former colleagues. They have stayed at the Croeso complex on a couple of occasions and are now seriously thinking about purchasing a property in North Wales and operating it as a management training centre. Jill has been Training Manager for a number of years and Stephen has been a Marketing Analyst for two leading travel companies. They have viewed a couple of potential old manor houses and have now become interested in purchasing a hotel which has only been built two years and is being sold off as part of a company reorganisation. Before they make an offer for the hotel Stephen and Jill need to know more about its financial performance to date. They have obtained the final accounts of the hotel and have asked you to analyse the figures and prepare a report for them on the business.

Profit and Loss Account for the year ended 5 April

		Year 1		Year 2
		£		£
Sales		655,000		825,000
Less cost of sales		230,000		350,000
		425,000		475,000
Less Expenses				
Wages	80,000		87,000	
Rates	34,000		38,000	
Interest payments	40,000		37,000	
Overheads	65,000	219,000	72,000	234,000
Net profit before loss		206,000		241,000

Balance Sheet as at 5 April

	Year 1	Year 2
Hotel	500,000	570,000
Fixtures and Fittings	290,000	304,000
Motor Vehicles	25,000	20,000
	815,000	894,000
Current Assets		
Stock	200,000	170,000
Debtors	170,000	150,000
Bank and cash	140,000	120,000
	1,325,000	1,334,000

Less Current Liabilities		
Creditors	400,000	350,000
Net assets	925,000	984,000
Financed by:		
Share capital ord. shares	450,000	600,000
Revaluation reserve		70,000
General reserve	50,000	225,000
Mortgage	425,000	89,000
Capital employed	925,000	984,000

4 Sarah and Kate are considering investing some of their savings in Falcan Leisure, a theme park. Their aim is to achieve capital growth on their investment, coupled with some income. They are considering purchasing shares in Falcon Leisure and have cut out a copy of the current year's figures on financial performance from the newspaper. They have asked you to advise them about the meaning of the terms used in the advertisement and whether or not Falcon Leisure is likely to be a good investment for their earnings.

Extract from comments by Lady Margaret Jamieson, in the Directors' Report

Your company goes from strength to strength as profits and earnings continue to grow.

Falcon Leisure: financial Performance	Year 3	Year 2	Year 1
Earnings per share	31p	27p	24p
Dividend yield	7p	6.2p	5.3p
Return on capital employed	39p	34p	28p
Dividend cover	2:1	2.5:1	3:1
Gross profit margin	16%	17%	15%
Net profit margin	6%	6.5%	6%
Gearing ratio	1.7:1	1.4:1	1:1

---

5 Sarah has been asked by the local Enterprise Club to give a presentation on "How to run a successful business". Although Sarah feels confident in presenting information on issues such as managing staff and marketing she is not confident when it comes to discussing aspects of financial management. Vanessa Rogers, the

Business Development Manager of the Enterprise Club, has particularly asked Sarah to focus on measuring financial performance as part of her talk. Sarah has asked you to prepare some notes that can be used in the presentation. She has asked you to write about 1,000 words, using the following headings:

- What do we mean by financial performance?
- How can measuring financial performance help us to run a successful business?
- What **five** key financial ratios can be used to measure business effectiveness?
- To what extent should we rely on what the ratios we analyse tell us?

---

6 Kate has been reading an article in the trade press about the risk of investment and has given you the following information on two companies in the travel industry – RoundTours and LuxTravel.

	RoundTours	LuxTravel
Called up share capital	100,000	50,00
Debentures	–	30,000
Unsecured loan stock	–	20,000
Capital employed	100,000	100,000
Return on capital employed	10%	15%
Earnings per share	12p	15p
Gross dividend	3p	5p
Average share price	£1.75	£2.20

Kate has asked the following questions:

---

(1) How are the companies geared?
(2) Are the companies safe to invest in?

---

17 Managing Working Capital

Cash flow problems

Many businesses experience **cash flow problems**. The difficulties they have to cope with from time to time include:

- Being unable to pay **suppliers' accounts** on time
- Being unable to gain the usual **discounts** from suppliers, due to small orders being placed and settling accounts late
- **Customers not settling their accounts** on time; and not
- Staying within an agreed **overdraft facility**.

In order to overcome these difficulties it is necessary to manage working capital effectively.

What is working capital and why is it important?

Working capital

Working capital is the difference between the **current assets** and the **current liabilities** of an organisation. In order to calculate this figure it is necessary to look at the Balance Sheet to find the current assets and current liabilities totals. In essence, working capital is the term used to describe a firm's **short-term use of funds**. A proportion of the organisation's capital will be tied up in fixed assets but a certain amount will be allocated to financing the day-to-day business expenditure. For example, money is required by the Croeso Hotel to purchase food and beverages, to pay wages, and to finance credit sales. If the firm does not possess enough working capital to meet its short-term obligations, it will be unable to continue trading.

Working capital management

The aim of working capital management is, therefore, to strike a balance between having **too much** or **too little**. Too much working capital means that a firm will earn a lower return on capital employed. Too little working capital, however, means that the business is in danger of ceasing to function altogether because it cannot generate the cash needed to finance its day-to-day trading.

Controlling working capital

In order to control the working capital of their business, managers need to analyse each element of their current assets and liabilities and decide what measures can be introduced to improve their overall working capital management. Within the **current assets** section of a Balance Sheet, the following items will usually appear:

> - Stock
> - Debtors
> - Cash at bank
> - Cash in hand

The current liabilities usually consist of the following elements:

> - Trade creditors
> - Taxation
> - Dividends payable
> - Bank overdraft

In order to improve the management of working capital it is essential to understand how each element of current assets listed above should be controlled; we shall take each in turn and then look at current liabilities.

Stock

Stock can take three different forms:

> - Raw materials
> - Work in progress
> - Finished goods

In the hospitality industry, food and beverages are the main stock items that are purchased. The majority of food purchases can be termed "raw materials" because they have to be **prepared** and **cooked** before they are sold to customers. Work in progress means those stock items which are **in the process of being turned** from raw materials into finished products: a factory will have goods which are not complete and therefore are not ready for sale, for example. Finished goods are those which are **available for sale** to customers.

It is important to remember that all stock has to be **financed**. Unless the goods are sold for cash the firm will have to finance its debtors. Only when the debtors finally pay will the business receive cash which can then be used to refinance the working capital cycle. The quicker the firm can produce and sell the goods, the faster the cash can be released to purchase more stock, thereby allowing the business to earn more profit.

The importance of an effective stock control system

Any business needs to be in the position where it has enough stock to meet customer demands. A fast food unit will lose sales revenue if it runs out of hamburgers, added to which customers will be very dissatisfied and may never return to the unit again. The fast food unit will similarly not want to carry a large stock of chicken nuggets if these are not a popular menu item, as they will be taking up valuable freezer space and may eventually have to be disposed of it they pass their sell-by date.

Holding stock is an expensive process. When food and beverages are delivered to a hospitality unit they have to be checked, transferred to the correct storage area, stored securely, counted and rotated regularly. Further costs are sometimes incurred if any stock is stolen, becomes obsolete, or becomes wastage.

A key stage, therefore, in designing an effective control system is determining the **correct levels of stock** to hold.

Stock levels

In order to make sure that stock is kept at its optimum level to meet daily demands it is necessary to set stock levels that take into account **usage rates** and the time taken to order new stocks and have them delivered, i.e., the **lead time**.

When deciding optimum stock levels for the Croeso Hotel's Victoria Restaurant, the **five** following factors should be taken into consideration:

> - The **average daily sales level** and anticipated **changes in demand**, e.g., the number of meals served in the restaurant per day
> - How **perishable** the stock items are – fresh fruit and vegetables will have a limited life
> - The average length of time it takes for **suppliers to deliver goods**
> - The **reliability** of suppliers
> - Estimated changes in **prices** and how this will offset demand.

There are **three** different stock levels that can be used:

> - Re-order level
> - Minimum stock level
> - Maximum stock level.

The **re-order stock level** is the amount **below which the stock must not fall**. The level is calculated as follows:

> Re-order level = Maximum usage × Maximum lead time

The **minimum stock level** is the **smallest amount** of stock which must be held, and it is a quantity **just below the re-order level**. Once this level is reached, stock must be purchased quickly if production is not to be stopped by a shortage of raw materials. The level is calculated as follows:

> Minimum stock level = Re-order level – (Average usage × Average lead time)

The **maximum stock level** is the **highest level** of stock which should be held. The level is calculated as follows:

Maximum stock level = Re-order level − (Minimum usage ×
Minimum lead time) + Re-order quantity

The Quick Munch sandwich bar: stock and re-order levels

The manager of the Quick Munch sandwich bar has been reviewing his
stock levels and he predicts the following usage rate of orange juice per
month:

	Cartons
Jan	120
Feb	120
Mar	130
Apr	150
May	200
Jun	300
Jul	400
Aug	500
Sep	450
Oct	300
Nov	150
Dec	120

The management has set the re-order quantity at 600 cartons and the
delivery times are:

Delivery time	Weeks
Maximum	4
Average	3
Minimum	2

To determine the Quick Munch's re-order, minimum and maximum
stock levels plus average stock levels for the next 12 months the following
calculations need to be carried out:

Re-order level = Maximum usage × Maximum lead time
500 cartons × 4 weeks = 2,000 cartons

Maximum level = Re-order Level − (Minimum usage × Minimum lead time) + Re-order quantity

2,000 cartons − (120 × 2) + 600 = 2,360 cartons

Minimum level = Re-order level − (Average usage × Average lead time)

2,000 cartons − (245 × 3) = 1,265 cartons

Average stock level = Minimum stock level + ½ Re-order quantity
= 1,265 + (ROQ $\underline{600}$) = 300
  2
= 1,265 cartons + 300 = 1565 cartons

Debtors

When selling goods and services to customers it is unlikely that they will all pay for their purchases immediately. Organisations thus become involved in selling goods and services **on credit**. These customers are often referred to as "trade debtors". Companies are usually content to offer credit to their customers as they realise the importance of offering terms which are as good as those offered by their competitors. However, firms should be cautious when extending credit to customers, because in doing so they may put considerable strain on their own **working capital**: a company may find that it cannot pay its own bills because it has not received payment from some customers.

Problems in allowing trade credit

There are two inherent problems in allowing trade credit to customers:

- Customers may take a **long time** to settle their debts
- Some customers may **never** pay their accounts, and as a result become **bad debts**.

Selling on credit enables the firm to increase its level of sales, but at the risk that some of the sales will turn out to be bad debts.

Credit control policy

In order to manage debtors effectively, organisations need to develop a credit control policy. One way of controlling debtors is to limit the length of time they are given to settle their outstanding accounts. In order to encourage prompt payment some companies offer a **cash discount**. This means that the quicker the customer pays an outstanding account the greater the discount they receive. For example, a 2½% discount may be offered for payment received within 10 days of the invoice being sent. Another way to ensure that customers pay their bills is to **remind** them regularly with letters and telephone calls. To achieve this, the company needs to keep an **up-to-date record system** of credit customers.

Debt factoring

In circumstances where customers take a long time to pay their debts some firms employ the services of a **debt factoring house**. They sell their unpaid invoices to the factoring house, which in turn credits the company's bank account with an agreed percentage of the invoice total and takes a percentage for this service. Although this is an expensive way of having debts settled it can be a useful method for small fast-growing businesses who are often short of working capital.

Credit references

It is also important to realise that credit does not have to be extended to **all** customers. One way of avoiding credit sales becoming bad debts is to check the creditworthiness of potential customers by asking for references from other suppliers, reviewing the past financial performance of the company, and enquiring with the bank about the firm's financial position. This process will usually result in **credit limits** being set for potential customers.

Debtors and cash flow

Whenever interest rates rise, credit controllers find it more difficult to collect their debts. Firms that are short of cash try to delay their payments, and such delays are often the first indication that a company is experiencing financial difficulties.

Cash and bank balances

If a business is to survive it must be able to generate its own cash by selling its products or services at a profit. Even if the firm is successful in this respect the management must ensure that the business has an **even flow of cash** so that it can always meet its liabilities.

Forecasting cash receipts and cash payments

The real problem is the **timing difference** between cash **receipts** and cash **payments**. If the business suffers from a seasonal sales pattern, as happens to many hotels, management must conserve cash resources during the months of lower sales. This is done by preparing forecasts showing the expected timing of cash receipts and cash payments. Cash forecasting is a difficult task, for it must take account of economic trading conditions, the firm's operating level and its policies relating to stock and credit control. Inflation will increase stockholding costs and other expenses, which can lead to liquidity problems: the business is having to finance these extra costs even though its trading and cash resources are the same as the previous year.

Cash holding levels

The aim must be to hold **sufficient cash to meet liabilities**. If too much cash is held lower returns will be made, which will depress profits and earnings. Any surplus should be invested in interest-earning deposits.

Overdraft facilities

If the firm is experiencing greater cash outflows than inflows, its survival will be in jeopardy unless it can obtain additional outside finance. The main source is the **bank overdraft**, but this should only be used to fund short-term cash deficits brought about by the seasonal nature of trade. The finance then becomes self-redeeming, and there is no danger of the business becoming **dependent on short-term borrowed funds** to meet its immediate liabilities.

Current liabilities

Money owed by the firm

Accountants refer to any sums of money which are owed by the firm as the current liabilities of the business. Whenever goods or services are bought on credit the firm receives a benefit while not having immediately to part with its own cash resources. In this way, the firm receives **interest-free credit** and thus will allow a higher level of trading than would have been possible if the firm had to pay for everything on a cash basis.

Cash holding levels

The key to managing current liabilities lies, as we saw above, in having sufficient cash to meet them **as and when they fall due for payment**. If this cannot be done there is a danger that too much of the firm's current assets will be financed by short-term lenders. This makes the firm financially unstable and can lead to a range of financial problems as creditors refuse to supply further goods or decide to take legal action to recover their money. Once the creditworthiness of a business has been damaged it will need greater cash resources in order to restore confidence by settling payments promptly. If this cannot be achieved the business will be in grave danger of being forced into receivership as creditors seek to limit the extent of their losses.

The working capital cycle

Look at Figure 17.1.

Figure 17.1   Model of an ideal cash operating cycle

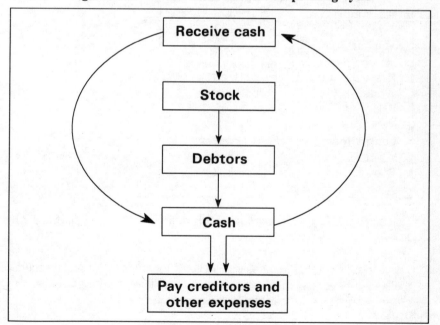

Effective management of the working capital cycle is a constant task. As the business trades each day the cycle is continually changing – stocks will be used and purchased, debtors increased, with some paying their balances, and more goods will be supplied on credit, with some creditors being paid. In spite of all these changes, the firm's cash resources must be sufficient to fund all these operations and so management must constantly **monitor** the cash receipts and payments of the business, with the aim of controlling the firm's cash operating cycle.

Study tasks

1 What is meant by the term "working capital", and why is it so important that Sarah and Kate manage the Croeso Hotel's working capital effectively?

2 The Croeso Hotel's Valley View bar stocks two bottles of house wine, one red and the other white. The usage quantities, re-order quantities and lead times are shown below:

Usage	litres per week
Maximum	300
Average	200
Minimum	100

Re-order quantity	Litres
White	1,000
Red	1,250

Lead time	Weeks
White	3–4
Red	2–3

Calculate the hotel's maximum, and minimum stock levels for each wine.

3 The Croeso Hotel's Gymnasium sells a high-protein drink to customers who have just completed a work-out. The usage quantities, re-order quantities and lead times are shown below:

Usage	Packets per week
Maximum	150
Average	100
Minimum	50
	Packets
Re-order quantity	500
	Weeks
Lead time	2–4

Calculate the Gymnasium's re-order level, maximum, minimum and average stock levels.

4 Sarah and Kate are considering altering their credit terms in order to increase sales. They currently offer a 2% discount for payments within 14 days, otherwise the account must be settled in full within 30 days.

The two women are considering offering 2% for payment within 30 days or settlement in full within 60 days. Prepare a statement showing the costs of:

> (1) The current credit terms
> (2) The proposed terms

assuming a customer owes £100.

5 Outline the procedures which Sarah and Kate should follow before giving any of their customers credit.

6 Show, by means of a diagram like that in Figure 17.1, the Croeso Hotel's cash operating cycle, and explain how the credit terms the hotel offers will affect the cycle.

18 Appraising Capital Investment Programmes

Investment for growth

Most businesses aim to **grow** in terms of their sales, market share and profits. As firms now have to operate in the global marketplace they have to be increasingly competitive with other international companies in their industry. One way of achieving these goals is through **investment**. This can take **two** forms.

Some organisations will need to **replace existing fixed assets** which have become either worn out or obsolete due to changes in technology. A conference centre may need to refurbish its seminar rooms with video conferencing facilities and a travel agency may need to update its computerised booking service.

A company may decide to invest in **additional fixed assets** in order to increase the productive capacity of the business. The management of a marina may invest in further yacht moorings which will increase revenue.

Capital rationing

Ideally, management should be able to invest in any new project where they believe a return can be earned. Unfortunately most businesses lack the financial resources to achieve all of their investment plans. It is therefore, necessary for them to choose or prioritise their investments. Such a process is referred to as capital rationing.

Factors to be assessed among competing investments

In any situation where a choice must be made for available funds between competing investments, management need to assess:

- Initial cost of the investment
- Degree of risk involved
- Estimated life cycle of the investment
- Estimated financial returns.

Methods of project assessment

There are **four** main methods of assessing capital investment projects:

- Pay back
- Accounting rate of return (ARR)
- Investment net present value (NPV), which considers the **time value** of money
- Internal rate of return (IRR).

All of these methods appraise the financial implications of investing in particular projects. In theory, if the investment does not meet the desired financial return, it should be rejected. We shall examine each in turn.

Pay back

Pay back calculations: Shapers Gymnasium

Many businesses need to know how quickly an investment pays for itself by generating sufficient cash flows to cover the initial outlay of money. Shapers Gymnasium is considering investing £30,000 in new weightlifting apparatus. The pay back time is calculated as follows:

$$\text{Pay back} = \frac{\text{Investment}}{\text{Cash flow per annum}}$$

Shapers Gymnasium's cash flow movements will show how the formula can be used:

Cash outflow £30,000 (Initial investment)

Cash inflows	
Year	£
1	6,000
2	10,000
3	14,000
Total inflows	30,000

The cash flows when added up for the 3 years exactly equal the £30,000 capital investment, and so the pay back time is exactly 3 years.

Pay back and cash shortfall: The Fun Time Theme Park

Generally, however, the pay back time will not work out precisely and so the exact time in years and months has to be calculated. This is shown in the cash flow movements of The Fun Time Theme Park:

The Fun Time Theme Park is considering investing £50,000 in a new water tunnel. The projected cash inflows are:

Cash inflows	
Year	£
1	10,000
2	25,000
3	30,000
4	35,000

When calculating the pay back time it is helpful to draw up a table:

Time	Cash Inflows	Total Inflows	Initial Investment
(Years)	£	£	£
0	–	–	50,000
1	10,000	10,000	–
2	25,000	35,000	–
3	30,000	65,000	

By adding up the cash inflows we can see that at the end of Year 2 the Theme Park has received £35,000 but that at the end of Year 3 total cash inflows are £65,000. The pay back time therefore occurs sometime between Year 2 and Year 3, which we must now calculate.

If the Year 3's cash inflow is added to the total inflows figure it will exceed the original investment, and so we must calculate the amount of money which needs to be earned to equal the intial investment. This sum may be referred to as the "cash shortfall", and is calculated as follows:

	£
Initial investment	50,000
Cash inflows	35,000
Shortfall	15,000

An assumption is now made that the cash inflows in Year 3 will be regular. As a result Year 3's cash inflows are divided by 12 to provide a monthly figure. The shortfall is then divided by this monthly amount so that the exact pay back time in years and months can be calculated:

Shortfall   £15,000

Cash flow Year 3
£30,000/ 12 = £2,500

$$\frac{\text{Shortfall}}{\text{Monthly Inflow}} \quad \frac{£15,000}{£2,500} = 6 \text{ months}$$

The pay back time for the new investment is therefore 2 years and 6 months.

Value and limitations of pay back

The pay back method of investment appraisal is the one most often used because it is relatively easy to calculate.

Its real value, however, lies in its ability to provide an **initial screening process** so that those projects which never pay for themselves are excluded unless there are other important criteria (such as safety requirements) which necessitate the investment. Complying with fire safety measures will be a legal requirement for the Croeso Hotel, and so the pay back time is irrelevant as the expenditure has to be incurred for the business to continue trading.

Finally, the quicker an investment pays for itself the less risk is involved as changes in consumer tastes or new technology may well adversely affect predicted future cash flows. Malt whisky must mature for 10 years, for example, and so there is a risk to the distillery that the demand for malt whisky in 10 years' time may have decreased due to changes in consumer taste. Blended whisky, on the other hand, matures much quicker thereby making it easier to predict consumer demand. In such cases projects which **pay for themselves quickly** are less risky.

A major limitation of the pay back method is that it tends to focus on the short rather than the long term, for once the pay back time has been calculated **future cash flows** are ignored. There is therefore a danger that a project may be chosen in preference to another just because it has a quick pay back time while another with a slower time may in fact have a longer life with greater cash inflows.

The accounting rate of return

Capital is a scarce resource and money invested in one project **cannot be invested in another**. Many firms try to maximise the return which they earn from their capital, and therefore select investments which will generate high returns.

Percentage return

The Accounting Rate of Return (ARR) method of appraisal calculates the percentage return which the new investment will yield, and is calculated as follows:

$$ARR = \frac{\text{Average net profit (after depreciation)}}{\text{Capital investment}} \times 100$$

Average net profit

The average net profit is found by subtracting the capital investment from the inflows and dividing this figure by the number of years the investment is expected to last.

30% ARR: The Dolphin Leisure Centre

The Dolphin Leisure Centre is considering investing £80,000 in a new squash court. The projected cash inflows are:

Year	£		£
1	25,000	Total inflows	200,000
2	30,000		
3	36,000	Less Investment	80,000
4	43,000		
5	66,000	Profit	120,000
Total inflows	200,000		

$$\text{Average profit} = \frac{\text{Profit}}{5 \text{ years}} = \frac{£120,000}{5 \text{ years}} = £24,000$$

$$\text{Accounting Rate of Return} = \frac{\text{Average profit} \times 100}{\text{Investment}}$$

$$\frac{£24,000 \times 100}{£80,000} = 30\%$$

The Dolphin Leisure Centre will earn a return of 30% on its initial investment.

Value and limitations of ARR

The ARR method of project appraisal is based on accounting profits and shows management immediately the likely financial returns from their investment.

There are however, three limitations with this approach. Firstly it is based on **averages**, and so high or low cash flows will distort the calculation of average profits. Secondly the method takes no account of the **size** of the investment and so a 10% return on £1,000 may be acceptable whereas it would probably be unacceptable on an investment of £1 million. Finally, as with the pay back method ARR does not take into account the **life time** of the project and therefore makes **comparisons** difficult in situations where investments have different life cycles.

Discounted cash flow

The time value of an investment

From a financial viewpoint money is said to have a time value because it can earn **interest**. If an investor has a sum of money and lends it to a bank, the investment will grow so long as the initial investment and the interest is not withdrawn. In such cases, the interest is **added** to the capital so that the investor earns interest on the total sum. This is called "compounding" and by using compound interest tables it is possible to calculate the **future value** of a sum of money if it could earn a certain return for a set number of years.

The compounding principle is important when considering an investment decision because if the cash inflows which will result from the investment could be received immediately, they could be invested to earn interest. Unfortunately this is not possible and so the cash inflows received in the future have lost the interest which they could have earned, and as a result an allowance must be made for this. This is done by using **discount tables** which work the opposite way to compound tables. As a result, once the cash inflows have been discounted they will become smaller, thereby taking into account the interest lost because of the time delay in receiving them.

Calculating the discounted cash flow from an investment

The actual discounted cash flow (DCF) calculation is very straightforward provided one has a set of discount tables. The figures can be calculated arithmetically but tables make the task easier. Today with the advent of spreadsheets many people prefer to use their computer which can perform the necessary calculations in seconds.

The cash flow table

The relevant tables are found on p. 240, but before they can be used it is best to draw what is called a **cash flow table**. This records the **receipts** and **outflows** of cash, together with the value placed on money, which is called the **discount factor** (d/f, see below). The discount factor is best thought of as the **rate of interest lost**, and will be determined by management. Once the cash inflows have been adjusted for the lost interest they are referred to as the **Net Present Value** (NPV). Figure 18.1 shows a blank cash flow table, which we shall then complete by using the figures for Occasions, a marquee hire company.

Figure 18.1 Cash flow table

Year	Cash inflow	Cash outflow	Net cash flow	D/F	NPV

Occasions: estimated cash flows

Occasions company are considering investing £60,000 in a new marquee. The cash inflows are shown below and the directors are not prepared to invest unless the investment can earn a **12% return**. The estimated cash flows are:

Year	£
1	25,000
2	33,000
3	45,000
4	62,000
5	70,000

Occasions: cash flow table

The investment will have a life of 5 years because there are cash inflows for 5 years and the discount factor will be 12% because that is the rate of return the directors require from their investment. A cash flow table can now be prepared, as in Figure 18.2.

Figure 18.2　Occasions: cash inflow, outflow and net cash flow

Year	Cash inflow	Cash outflow	Net cash flow	D/F	NPV
	£	£	£		£
0	–	60,000	60,000	12	(60,000)
1	25,000	–	25,000		
2	33,000		33,000		
3	45,000		45,000		
4	62,000		62,000		
5	70,000		70,000		

Figure 18.2 shows the time period and the cash inflows and cash outflows. The time period begins in Year 0 when the initial investment of £60,000 is made. This sum is still worth £60,000 because the investment has just been made and so no interest has been lost. It is shown in brackets because, it must be **subtracted** later on from the total of the cash inflows, NPV.

Occasions' cash inflow is the same as the net cash inflow but if the company has to invest an additional £10,000 in Year 1 then this would have to be **deducted** from the cash inflow, and this is why Figure 18.2 shows the **net cash flow**.

Using the discount factor

So far, the discount factor has not been explained. The tables on p. 240 show the NPV of a unit of currency, and the relevant figures for a discount factor of 12% are shown below:

Year	NPV £
0	1.000
1	0.893
2	0.797
3	0.712
4	0.636
5	0.567

We next need to insert these figures under the heading "discount factor". Finally, by multiplying the net cash flow figure by the discount factor, we arrive at its NPV. We can do this for Occasions' cash flow movements; our table will look like that in Figure 18.3.

Figure 18.3   Occasions: NPV calculations

Year	Cash inflow	Cash outflow	Net cash flow	D/F	NPV
	£	£	£		£
0	–	(60,000)	(60,000)	12	(60,000)
1	25,000	–	25,000	0.893	22,325
2	33,000		33,000	0.797	26,301
3	45,000		45,000	0.712	32,040
4	62,000		62,000	0.636	39,432
5	70,000		70,000	0.567	39,690
					99,788

The balance of £99,788 is calculated by adding up the NPV of all the cash flows and subtracting the initial investment from them:

	£
Total discounted inflows	159,788
Initial investment	60,000
NPV	99,788

If the discounted cash flows **exceed** the investment then the investment meets the desired return. If the discounted cash flows are **less** then the investment fails to do this, and in the absence of other criteria the investment would not go ahead because it cannot earn the required return.

Value and limitations of DCF

The main advantage of the DCF method is that it considers the **time value of money**, so that the value of money received in the **future** can be compared with **present** sums.

It is, however, often difficult to assess what the cost of money **should be**: different rates will inevitably produce different results. Discounting is also a concept which non-financial managers may find difficult to understand.

Internal rate of return

The IRR method is really a further refinement of discounting cash flows. Once an investment yields a **positive** NPV a higher discount factor is applied until the discounted value of the cash inflows equals the cash outflow. The NPV is then zero, and this is the IRR.

Attempting to lessen risk

Pay back, ARR and NPV all seek to lessen the risk of investing in projects which cannot yield a financial return. Unfortunately all of these methods require predictions about future returns, and these cannot be made with certainty. If this data is wrong, or costs and cash flows suddenly change because of unpredicted inflation or market trends brought about by technological or social change, the actual returns may prove to be very different from those expected.

Study tasks

1 Sarah and Kate are considering investing money in the Croeso Hotel grounds by planting more trees and shrubs. They have been quoted £1,500 from a local firm and are wondering whether or not they should proceed with the investment. What factors should Sarah and Kate take into account before making this investment decision?

2 Hugh Roberts, the Croeso Hotel's Head Chef, has requested a new food mixer, dish washer and deep freeze. The costs and cash flows for each piece of capital equipment are as shown:

	Food mixer £	Dish washer £	Deep freeze £
Investment	450	1,200	1,700
Cash inflows			
Year			
1	260	450	300
2	410	600	450
3	550	800	500
4	600	850	700

Calculate the pay back time for each piece of equipment.

3 The Croeso Hotel is considering purchasing a fax machine which will be available for guest use. The cost and projected cash flows are shown below:

	£
Fax machine	2,500
Cash flow	
Year	
1	900
2	1,200
3	1,600

Calculate the accounting rate of return (ARR) which the new project can earn.

4 The Croeso Hotel is considering investing in projects which will yield the cash returns listed below in the future. Calculate their value, and write a memo demonstrating in detail why management should always consider the **time value** of money before making investment decisions:

Time (years)	Discount factor (%)	Sum to be received £
1	10	3,000
4	12	10,000
6	8	5,000
9	14	60,000
3	20	20,000
15	16	44,000

5 Sarah and Kate are considering investing in a new computerised reservations system for the Croeso Hotel. The costs, cash flows and savings from the investment are shown below:

Year	Investment £	Cash inflow £	Savings £	Taxation £
0	25,000	–	–	–
1	1,500	9,000	1,200	500
2	2,000	14,000	2,000	700
3	500	16,000	1,000	950
4	–	20,000	1,000	1,400

If the Croeso Hotel's cost of capital is 12%, calculate whether or not this investment has a positive or a negative NPV.

6 Sarah and Kate have now been advised that in planning their investment in a computerised reservations system they have not taken the effects of inflation into account, and that they should not invest unless it can earn a 16% return. Using the net cash flows from Question 5, calculate whether or not this investment can in fact earn the required return.

19   Raising Finance

Sources and costs of capital for growth

There are many different ways in which a firm may **finance itself**. The money may come either from the owners who are the shareholders, or from creditors who are lenders of funds to the business. The exact proportion of finance provided from each source will differ from industry to industry, and from firm to firm. Most businesses, however, will be financed by a mixture of share and loan capital.

Some businesses are said to be **capital-intensive** because a lot of money is needed to finance their fixed assets. The Croeso Hotel and its leisure centre requires large amounts of money to finance the land, buildings and equipment necessary for it to function. Before raising money, management must compare and contrast the various sources and costs of capital available.

Although organisations need funds before they can commence trading, they also need additional capital injections to support planned expansion and growth. This results in the firm either increasing the percentage of share capital or loan capital financing the business. Once again, it is necessary to evaluate the various sources and costs of capital so that the business has a sound financial base.

Internal sources of capital: retained profits

Before additional capital is sought management should review their own **internal sources of funds**. Most new investment is financed from retained profits: if the profits are not distributed to the shareholders as dividend they can be ploughed back into the firm. This money can then be used to finance the necessary capital expenditure which will help the business to achieve such goals as increasing market share.

Unfortunately using retained profits is a slow process because it is unlikely that they will be able to keep pace with the large amounts of capital needed to finance the investment programme. This is particularly true if the market is growing very fast and becoming increasingly competitive. In such situations, **outside sources** of finance will be required.

External sources of funds

Raising additional share capital

Stock Exchange quotation

If the **existing shareholders** have seen a steady growth in profits and dividends they may be prepared to invest more money. If the firm decides to offer more shares, provided it is a public limited company (plc) these could be sold by issuing a **prospectus** and inviting the general public to subscribe for them. In this way the firm's capital base would be expanded.

Rights issue

While this method is open to any publicly quoted company it is an expensive process because of the number of Stock Exchange regulations. For this reason it is more usual for firms to raise additional share capital by what is called a "rights issue" or a "placing".

A rights issue occurs whenever a company allows existing shareholders to **purchase more shares based on their current ownership**. The rights issue may state "one new share for each four already held", in which case it is referred to as a "1 for 4" rights issue. Rights issues are cheaper than issuing a general prospectus and are usually popular with existing shareholders because the shares are sold at a lower price than that currently quoted on the stock market. There is also an added advantage for the company in that if the rights issue is taken up by all the shareholders the voting rights will be unaffected because shareholders will not increase their holding at the expense of others.

Merchant bank placing

Alternatively additional share capital could be raised by placing the shares with a city institution, usually a merchant bank. This means that the bank agrees to find buyers for the shares by approaching financial institutions such as insurance and pension companies.

Raising additional debt capital

While any of these methods will increase the equity capital of the business they are not really appropriate unless the company wishes to raise a substantial sum of money. In many cases companies require smaller sums and therefore decide to **borrow** the money because the costs of raising additional share capital would be excessive in relation to the funds needed.

Borrowed money, referred to as "debt capital", is a very flexible form of finance, in that it can be raised for just short-term purposes or for longer periods if necessary. It may also prove to be cheaper than equity finance, thereby reducing the firm's overall cost of capital.

Bank overdraft

This is one of the most popular forms of finance, and has the added advantage that the business only incurs interest on the **actual amount borrowed**. As payments into the bank will reduce the overdraft this makes it an attractive form of finance although it is technically repayable on demand. Overdraft finance, however, should only be used to fund short-term liquidity shortages. There is the added danger that interest rates cannot be fixed and so short-term increases in money market interest rates will make a firm's cost of borrowing more expensive.

Bank term loan

The main High Street banks have started to increase the amount of money which they are prepared to lend to industry over long periods of time. Such loans are called "term loans", their name deriving from the length of time which the loan is to last. A variety of **repayment options** are generally available, allowing companies to have interest-only loans with repayment of capital at the end of the loan, or repayments which include interest and capital. The former are attractive to companies short of cash because their investments will not generate large amounts of money until some years after the initial investment.

Factoring

If a business is expanding rapidly it usually finds itself short of cash, particularly if debtors delay payments. One way of financing this growth is to factor the debts to a factoring house. If this is done the company sells its invoices to the factoring house who pay a fixed percentage of the sum owed to the company immediately, and the balance at a later date after deducting their charges. Factoring is an expensive form of short-term finance because of the high percentages taken by the factoring companies, but it may prove an invaluable form of finance to fast-growing companies who have no other source of short-term finance.

Hire purchase

When a company enters into a hire purchase agreement it effectively agrees to rent an asset with an option to purchase it at the end of the term for a nominal amount of money. The money owed is shown as a liability in the Balance Sheet and the asset is shown in the Balance Sheet even though the option to purchase it has not yet been exercised. Hire purchase is generally an expensive form of finance, and its use has declined recently with the advent of **leasing** which has a number of tax and other financial advantages.

Leasing

Instead of purchasing an asset such as vehicles, computers or office equipment outright, they could be leased. A lease is a legal agreement between two parties, referred to as the **lessor** (the owner of the asset) and **lessee** (person leasing the asset) who have certain rights and obligations. For all practical purposes leasing can be thought of as renting. This is because during the lifetime of the contract the lessee never owns the asset. There are **two** main types of lease:

- **Operating lease**

  If the lessee enters into an operating lease the lessor agrees to provide the equipment and to repair and service it during the contract. At the end of the lease, which will be less than the life of the asset, the lessor can either lease it to another business or sell it. In most cases the lessor will be a finance house which specialises in this form of finance.

- **Finance lease**

  This type of lease still operates according to the general principles of leasing, but in such cases it normally lasts for the life of the asset and the lessee is responsible for the servicing and maintenance of the equipment. At the end of the leasing agreement the lessee may be able to enter into a secondary leasing agreement whereby the asset can be used for a nominal sum. In other cases, the lessee may be able to sell the asset on behalf of the lessor and keep most of the sale proceeds because the lessor will have recouped the capital outlay plus required profit during the lifetime of the first lease.

Mortgages and debentures

If a firm owns fixed assets such as property or land it is able to provide very good security for any money that it intends to borrow. There are two main legal documents, called **mortgages** and **debentures**, which show that the property or other assets have been offered as security for a loan. The loans will generally be for a long period of time, with fixed dates for interest and repayment of capital. Interest rates are usually lower than unsecured loans because the lender has less risk.

- **Mortgages** are usually taken out when the asset is offered as security to one lender such as a bank.
- **Debentures**, however, are offered for sale to investors in £100 units and are bought and sold on the Stock Exchange. In this way large firms are able to create a market for their debt securities. This makes them attractive to investors who may need to sell their debentures if they suddenly need cash. As a result debentures are generally only issued by large publicly quoted companies, whereas small firms can raise money by mortgaging their assets.

Sale and lease back

If a business has a freehold property it could sell it to an insurance company and at the same time enter into an agreement to lease back the property, thereby providing the business with a **capital sum**. This should only be done as a last resort, however, because the firm will have lost a valuable asset which could always be mortgaged. If the sale and lease back agreement contains frequent rent reviews, and if inflation is high, the true cost of the finance could work out to be very expensive.

Commercial paper

A £10 note is an example of commercial paper. It is issued by the government and entitles the holder to receive value. In the same way, publicly quoted companies can raise money by selling **financial instruments** which offer the holder a guaranteed rate of interest.

Very large companies can raise capital by selling debt securities in the capital markets, or by raising money short term in the money markets. Investors are prepared to purchase these financial instruments because of the creditworthiness of the companies involved. The term "junk bond" came into existence when companies of lower creditworthiness also began offering commercial paper. Junk bonds, however, were attractive to investors because of the very high interest rates offered which sought to compensate investors for the additional risk.

Managing the overall cost of capital

These different sources of funds illustrate the range of available finance which can be used by business. Money, like any other commodity, is a **scarce resource**, whose price is reflected in the interest cost of the capital. As a result it pays a firm to keep its overall cost of capital to a minimum. This means that the management must carefully assess the **length of time** the money is needed, the **cost** of the capital and how the additional debt capital will affect the firm's **creditworthiness**.

The level of a firm's borrowing

Burden of interest payments

Whenever, a firm raises additional money by borrowing it inevitably alters its **ratio of debt to equity capital**. Shareholders receive dividends if the firm makes sufficient profits. There is no legal duty for companies to pay dividends but they must meet their interest charges: the more debt capital a firm has, the greater the risk that it will be unable to meet all of its interest payments.

Impact on credit rating

Ultimately it is the **lender** who assesses whether or not too much money has been borrowed. As the amount of debt capital increases interest charges are likely to rise, thereby compensating lenders for the additional risk. Credit analysts assess companies' ability to meet their debt obligations in the light of economic trading conditions. They grade companies, with an AAA rating being the most highly prized status. Any downgrading in their credit rating will make a firm's commercial paper less attractive to investors. Firms therefore have to consider the impact on their **current credit rating** of increasing their debt capital.

Gearing

Credit analysts prefer to see companies financed mainly by its share-holders. It is they after all who own the business and so shareholders should provide the majority of the finance. The ratio of share capital to debt capital is referred to as gearing. A firm is said to be highly geared if it has a high proportion of debt capital to equity capital. The ratio of debt to equity capital is calculated by the ratio:

> Debt capital
> ―――――――――
> Equity capital

If the ratio is 1:1, which means that the business is financed by equal debt and equity capital, it is said to be **highly geared** because lenders have invested as much money in the business as the owners. The level of gearing will affect the firm's cost of borrowing because of the risk involved of the firm not being able to meet its interest payments.

The cost of debt capital and the tax implications of borrowing

The cost of debt capital is partly fixed by current market rates of interest plus the premium which is required for lending money to the business. The better the firm's credit rating the lower the premium, because it is seen as a good credit risk. A firm's credit rating is influenced chiefly by its ability to meet its current liabilities, which includes its debt interest and capital borrowed. The more debt capital a firm has, the greater the probability of it not being able to meet its interest payments if profits fall. This explains why lenders usually increase the interest rate premium to compensate for the extra risk. Nevertheless raising additional debt capital can offer a business important financial advantages:

- Interest payments are **tax-deductable**, and so as long as the business is profitable the tax advantage will reduce the cost of capital. If a company has borrowed a £100,000 at an interest rate of 16% interest payments are £16,000 a year, but if the company pays Corporation Tax at 50% its true interest cost will be reduced to £8,000.
- Dividend payments to shareholders, however, are **not tax-deductable**. This means that the firm must have sufficient cash resources to meet its dividend payments whilst not being able to offset the cost against its corporation tax liability.

The dividend which a company pays to its shareholders is in effect its **cost of equity capital**. Shareholders seek to maximise their wealth by seeing a constant increase in dividend payments coupled with an increase in the value of their shares. Companies which can pay high dividends generally enjoy higher share prices, thereby making them popular with shareholders who see the possibility of making capital gains from their investment.

The fewer the shareholders, the smaller the amount of money needed to pay dividends and in percentage terms these will be higher because they are shared by fewer people. This is shown by the figures for Company A and Company B:

	Company A £	Company B £
Share capital		
(£1 ordinary shares)	100,000	50,000
Loan capital	–	50,000
Capital employed	100,000	100,000

Companies A and B have the same net profit of £10,000, which is distributed as dividend to shareholders. Company A has 100,000 shares and so each shareholder receives 10p per share. The shareholders in Company B, however, receive 20p because there are only 50,000 of them.

Highly geared companies are therefore potentially able to pay higher dividends because any additional cash flows after paying loan interest will belong to the shareholders. If the directors chose to do so, they may be paid as dividends. Higher gearing also reduces the number of shareholders, and so there will be fewer of them to share the profits.

The weighted cost of capital

Many firms will have raised their long-term capital from shareholders and long-term lenders. By calculating the different proportions of capital which make up the capital base with their relative cost it is possible to work out the firm's weighted average cost of capital, often abbreviated to WACC. This is illustrated by the figures for The Star Theatre's cost of capital.

The Star Theatre: capital base and dividend payments

The Star Theatre's capital base of £100,000 is made up of both share and debt capital:

Capital employed

75,000 £1 Ordinary shares
25,000 12% Debenturs

The theatre's average dividend payment has been 16p per ordinary share and may be regarded as the cost of share capital. The cost of the loan capital is the 12% interest which must be paid to debenture holders. This is 3% less than the share capital. By borrowing the £25,000 instead of issuing more shares the company has been able to reduce its overall cost of capital.

The Star Theatre: weighted cost of capital

The theatre's weighted cost of capital can now be calculated:

Capital	Proportion	Cost	Cost × Proportion
		%	%
Shares	3/4	16	12
Debenture	1/4	12	3
Weighted average cost of capital			15

Loan capital and business growth

Whenever a firm can reduce its overall cost of capital by borrowing, it makes sense to do so. Debt capital is a very flexible form of finance and is more easily available than equity capital. Small firms find it easier to raise loan capital, and sometimes exceed prudent levels of borrowed funds because they cannot increase their share capital. Sometimes large firms also fall into this trap, particularly if they seek to finance their expansion with debt capital. Nevertheless properly used loan capital offers any business a number of financial advantages which should help it increase its profitability and return on capital employed.

Study tasks

1   Sarah and Kate are going to meet Lynn Harvey, their bank manager, to discuss additional loan finance which will be used for the computerised reservation system they were appraising in Chapter 18. What information should they take with them to support their case for a loan?

2   The hotel currently has credit sales of £30,000 a month. Credit terms are 30 days. The factor's fee would be 2.5% of sales and the factor would advance 80% of the invoice value of debtors immediately at an interest rate of 12 %. Calculate the interest cost of raising money this way.

3   For the last three months the Croeso Hotel has had an overdraft which has averaged £12,000 a month. The bank are currently charging 1.5% over their base rate which is 10.5% plus 30p a transaction. On average the hotel presents 100 cheques a month. Calculate the hotel's cost of overdraft finance. Assume a 30-day month.

4   Sarah and Kate are considering expanding the facilities currently offered in the Croeso Hotel's leisure centre. At first, they thought of a bank loan, but Lynn Harvey has hinted that such finance is hard to obtain at the moment. Prepare a short report outlining 2 different sources of finance available to them, including the advantages and disadvantages of each.

5   The Croeso Hotel's capital structure is made up of equity and debt capital:

> 250,000 £1 Ordinary shares
> 150,000 10% Bank term loan

The hotel is considering borrowing a further £100,000 from a finance house. The interest rate would be 16%. The shares currently pay a dividend of 12p per share:

> (a) Calculate the firm's current weighted cost of capital
> (b) Calculate the firm's weighted cost of capital if it takes out the additional loan.

6 Assuming that the Croeso Hotel takes the loan from the finance house (Question 5):

> **(a)** Calculate the new level of gearing
> **(b)** Write a report outlining how this new level of borrowing may affect the hotel's profitability and cash flow.

20 Managing Foreign Exchange

Exposure to exchange rate risk

The hospitality and leisure industries are both truly international. Tourists and business travellers come from all over the world on visits and holidays. Once they have arrived they have to be able to pay for the goods and services which they require. Their own currency is generally unacceptable, and so they need to be able to exchange their currency for that of the country they are visiting. This is done by creating a **market in foreign currencies** operated by the worlds' banks who are prepared to buy and sell currencies on behalf of their customers.

The rate quoted by the banks effectively determines the price of goods and services in one country relative to the cost in another. If a person receives a favourable rate of exchange they will obtain a large amount of money. The prices in that country will then seem cheap, whereas if only a small amount of foreign currency is received prices will seem high. A holidaymaker from Britain going to Switzerland will at present receive just over 2 Swiss francs for each £1 exchanged: Switzerland is thus an expensive place for British tourists to visit.

The travel and tourism industries are sensitive to fluctuations in exchange rates because any change in the rate immediately alters the price of goods and services in one currency relative to another.

In business there is always a risk of entering into a contract, but this risk is increased when contracts are made overseas: any change in the rate will alter the costs involved. These changes make it difficult for industry to know the exact cost or revenues that will be received. If the foreign exchange markets are very volatile a firm's profit margin could be lost by an adverse movement in the exchange rate. Managers therefore need to know not just how to **calculate** exchange rates, but also how to **limit** their **exposure to risk**.

What is an exchange rate?

For international trade to be able to take place, business people and tourists must be able to **buy** and **sell** different currencies of the world.

This process is carried out by means of a **market** which brings together buyers and sellers. The rate which each is prepared to buy and sell at is determined by the forces of supply and demand. This is how the price of any commodity is determined in a market, and foreign exchange is no exception.

Each weekday the foreign exchange markets trade the world's currencies. There is no one market place, for all dealing is conducted over the telephone from the dealing rooms in banks. Each working day the equivalent of 1 trillion US dollars is traded, making the foreign exchange market the largest in the world.

Whenever there are more sellers in the market than buyers, the price of the currency **falls**. If there are more buyers than sellers, the price **rises**. All day new prices are being established, and so the world's currencies are constantly changing in value in relation to each other. To help customers banks publish rates, normally each day, at which they will buy or sell currency.

How are exchange rates quoted?

The "spread" of rates

Banks make profits by buying and selling currencies. Although they charge customers commission, their main income comes from the difference between their **buying** and **selling rates**. For the banks to be able to make a profit they must have a higher buying price than their selling price. Whenever they buy currency from a customer they take as much of it as they can in exchange for the money which the customer wants. Likewise, when they sell it they give the customer the smallest amount possible. The difference between the buying and selling price is called the "spread". By setting buying and selling prices in this way banks are able to make a profit out of their foreign exchange dealings.

Buying high and selling low

Exchange rates are quoted on the London Market in the form of a table like this:

Sterling spot and forward rates

	Range	Close	1 Month	3 Month
New York	1.8135–1.8215	1.8155–1.8165	1.06–1.05pr	2.90–2.88pr
Frankfurt	2.5158–2.5268	2.5162–2.5196	1.5–1pr	27/8–25/8pr
Tokyo	223.25–225.27	223.32–223.65	11/8–1pr	3.5–3pr

At first sight our table looks very confusing because not only are a number of different rates quoted but each column shows **two** different exchange rates for the currency. The first principle to remember is that banks quote the rates **from their own standpoint**. This means that all transactions are seen from their own accounting records and not from those of their customers. If a customer wishes to exchange dollars for pounds, then the bank is being asked to **buy dollars** from the customer and then **sell** them **pounds**.

It is important to remember the old maxim which we have already seen: banks **buy high** and **sell low**, and so they will use the higher rate when buying dollars from the customer and the lower rate when selling pounds. In this way they will buy as many dollars as possible whilst managing to give away as little as possible of their own currency. Once this general principle is understood the rest of our table can be simply explained.

The day's spread

This shows how the exchange rate **altered during the day**. It will show the lowest and highest rates quoted during yesterday's trading. In our table above the pound traded against the US dollar at 1.8135–1.8215. This means that during the day's trading the bank was prepared to sell dollars at 1.8135 and buy them at 1.8215.

The close

This shows the exchange rates being quoted at the close of trading: in our case 1.8155–1.8165.

1 month and 3 months: forward contracts

The banks are prepared to offer rates for customers who wish to take delivery or sell foreign currency in 1 or 3 months' time. These contracts are referred to as "forward contracts", and they enable the customer to **fix a rate beforehand**. Unlike the spot rate forward rates are not quoted, and have to be calculated by deducting the premium and adding the discount to the spot rate.

Entering into forward contracts can be beneficial if it is likely that there will be a sudden change in rates, as happened when sterling left the Exchange Rate Mechanism (ERM) in September 1992. An importer buying German cars would have received 2.95 marks for each pound prior to sterling's devaluation. Once sterling was devalued the importer would receive fewer marks for each pound exchanged, and so the cost of the cars would rise. If this price increase could not be passed on to customers then a loss would be made. If the importer had entered into a forward contract, the exchange rate would have been fixed beforehand and any subsequent change in rate would not have affected the importer.

Exchange rate arithmetic

By using the rates quoted in our table the cost of foreign goods or the amount of money to be received from exporting goods can be calculated.

Spot rate

If the contract is to be made immediately we will use the spot rate, which is the rate **currently being quoted** by dealers in the foreign exchange market.

Brook's Tours: US accommodation

Brook's Tours have to pay for accommodation in America. They owe a hotel $100,000. The sterling cost can be calculated by dividing the sum owed by the bank's spot rate for selling currency to customers:

$$\frac{\$100,000}{\pounds = \$1.8155} = \pounds55,081.24 \text{ (sum payable)}$$

Once again it is important to remember that the transaction is always calculated from the standpoint of the **bank's trading position**. When a customer wants to buy currency the bank sells it, and so the lower rate is used. This is because banks always use the lower rate for selling currency and the higher rate for buying.

If Brook's Travel were to receive 60,000 US dollars in payment for holidays booked in the United Kingdom, the bank's **buying rate** would be used:

$$\frac{\$60,000}{£ = \$1.8165} = £33,030.55 \text{ (sum received)}$$

Forward rate

The forward rate is calculated from the spot rate. The difference between the spot rate and the forward rate arises because of different interest rates charged for money by the world's financial markets. The fact that a currency is shown either as being at a premium or a discount should not be taken as an indication of how exchange rates are likely to move during the time span of the forward contract. Whenever the forward rate is shown at a premium this must be **deducted** from the spot rate and if it is shown at a discount it must be **added**. The premium makes the currency more expensive whilst the discount reduces the cost.

Travel Wise: planning foreign exchange needs

Travel Wise is considering entering into a 3-month forward contract. The spot rate is 1.8155–1.8165 and the 3-month forward rate is 2.90 cpm–2.88 cpm (the letters cpm mean cents premium). The forward rate can now be calculated by deducting the premium from the spot rate:

3-month forward rate

	Bank's selling rate	Bank's buying rate
Spot rate	1.8155	1.8165
Less premium	0.0290	0.0288
Forward rate	1.7865	1.7877

Option contracts

These contracts also allow business people to plan their foreign exchange transactions. Unlike forward contracts the buyer has the right, but not the obligation, to buy or sell foreign currency at a specified rate and time period. By entering into a **put** option the purchaser has the right to **sell**, whereas a **call** option gives the buyer the right to **purchase** the option. A **double option** gives the buyer the right to **buy** or **sell**.

Option contracts are a flexible way of seeking protection from exchange rate movements because the buyer of the option does **not have to take it up**. If the rate is unfavourable the only money lost is the cost of the option, but if it is advantageous the option can be exercised. As a result option contracts are a very flexible way of avoiding exchange rate risk and are often used as part of a firm's **hedging strategy**.

Hedging exchange rate risk

The word "hedging" is used to describe strategies which firms use to mitigate the risks of entering into foreign exchange contracts. Two of the main "hedges" used by companies are the forward and option contracts we have considered above. A "perfect hedge" is one where the possibility of future gain or loss has been **eliminated**.

Risk taking or risk avoiding strategies

Throughout this book we have seen that the financial manager's basic resource is **money**, and that this scarce resource must be deployed to achieve the maximum return for the business. By appreciating the nature and principles of both business and financial risk a strategy can be developed which will be consistent with the firm's overall objectives of being either a risk taker or a risk avoider.

Study tasks

1 A number of foreign guests at the Croeso Hotel have asked to change currency. The amounts and the current rates are shown below. Calculate how much sterling must be paid out by the hotel cashier.

Currency	Amount	Exchange rate
German DM	800	2.43–2.45
US$	1,000	1.51–1.54
French Franc	700	8.05–8.76
Swiss Franc	900	2.10–2.40
Dutch Guilder	2,000	3.20–3.50

2 Kate is visiting Germany, Switzerland and France to promote the Croeso Hotel. She has decided to take the following amounts of foreign currency. Calculate her sterling cost.

Currency	Amount	Exchange rate
German DM	2,000	2.39–2.40
Swiss Franc	1,000	2.00–2.12
French Franc	800	8.50–9.23

3 Sarah and Kate are considering purchasing some German wines for the Croeso Hotel's cellar. The vineyards must be paid in Deutsche Marks as soon as the wines are delivered. What are the **three** risks which the hotel is exposed to in this transaction?

4 Kate has just seen the morning papers and the headline in one of them reads "More uncertainty as dollar continues to slide". Why do foreign exchange rates alter, and what "hedging strategies" can the Croeso Hotel take to minimise their effect?

5 The Croeso Hotel has purchased some specialist software from an American supplier. The cost is $3,000 which will be due in 3 months' time. Sarah and Kate have decided to enter into a forward contract. The spot rate and premium are:

Spot rate £1.7550 3 months 0.07cpm

(a) Calculate the sterling cost of the software if they enter into a forward contract.

(b) Explain how this reduces exchange rate risk.

6 For the last 6 months sterling has been appreciating on the foreign exchange markets. The hotel is receiving $4,000 next month from an American tour company. The spot rate and premium are:

Spot rate 1.7530 3 months 0.11cpm

(a) Calculate the amount of sterling which the hotel will receive.

(b) Explain why in such a situation it may be beneficial to enter into a forward contract.

Appendix: NPV tables

Present value of £1 (PVIF)$P = S(1 + r)^{-n}$

Period	1%	2%	3%	4%	5%	6%	7%	8%	9%	10%	12%	14%	15%
1	0.990	0.980	0.971	0.962	0.952	0.943	0.935	0.926	0.917	0.909	0.893	0.877	0.870
2	0.980	0.961	0.943	0.925	0.907	0.890	0.873	0.857	0.842	0.824	0.797	0.769	0.756
3	0.971	0.942	0.915	0.889	0.864	0.840	0.816	0.794	0.772	0.751	0.712	0.675	0.658
4	0.961	0.924	0.889	0.855	0.823	0.792	0.763	0.735	0.708	0.683	0.636	0.592	0.572
5	0.951	0.906	0.863	0.822	0.784	0.747	0.713	0.681	0.650	0.621	0.567	0.519	0.497
6	0.942	0.888	0.838	0.790	0.746	0.705	0.666	0.630	0.596	0.564	0.507	0.456	0.432
7	0.933	0.871	0.813	0.760	0.711	0.665	0.623	0.583	0.547	0.513	0.452	0.400	0.376
8	0.923	0.853	0.789	0.731	0.677	0.627	0.582	0.540	0.502	0.467	0.404	0.351	0.327
9	0.914	0.837	0.766	0.703	0.645	0.592	0.544	0.500	0.460	0.424	0.361	0.308	0.284
10	0.905	0.820	0.744	0.676	0.614	0.558	0.508	0.463	0.422	0.386	0.322	0.270	0.247
11	0.896	0.804	0.722	0.650	0.585	0.527	0.475	0.429	0.388	0.350	0.287	0.237	0.215
12	0.887	0.788	0.701	0.625	0.557	0.497	0.444	0.397	0.356	0.319	0.257	0.208	0.187
13	0.879	0.773	0.681	0.601	0.530	0.469	0.415	0.368	0.326	0.290	0.229	0.182	0.163
14	0.870	0.758	0.661	0.577	0.505	0.442	0.388	0.340	0.299	0.263	0.205	0.160	0.141
15	0.861	0.743	0.642	0.555	0.481	0.417	0.362	0.315	0.275	0.239	0.183	0.140	0.123
16	0.853	0.728	0.623	0.534	0.458	0.394	0.339	0.292	0.252	0.218	0.163	0.123	0.107
17	0.844	0.714	0.605	0.513	0.436	0.371	0.317	0.270	0.231	0.198	0.146	0.108	0.093
18	0.836	0.700	0.587	0.494	0.416	0.350	0.296	0.250	0.212	0.180	0.130	0.095	0.081
19	0.828	0.686	0.570	0.475	0.396	0.331	0.276	0.232	0.194	0.164	0.116	0.083	0.070
20	0.820	0.673	0.554	0.456	0.377	0.312	0.258	0.215	0.178	0.149	0.104	0.073	0.061
25	0.780	0.610	0.478	0.375	0.295	0.233	0.184	0.146	0.116	0.092	0.059	0.038	0.030
30	0.742	0.552	0.412	0.308	0.231	0.174	0.131	0.099	0.075	0.057	0.033	0.020	0.015

Period	16%	18%	20%	24%	28%	32%	36%	40%	50%	60%	70%	80%	90%
1	0.862	0.847	0.833	0.806	0.781	0.758	0.735	0.714	0.667	0.625	0.588	0.556	0.526
2	0.743	0.718	0.694	0.650	0.610	0.574	0.541	0.510	0.444	0.391	0.346	0.309	0.277
3	0.641	0.609	0.579	0.524	0.477	0.435	0.398	0.364	0.296	0.244	0.204	0.171	0.146
4	0.552	0.516	0.482	0.423	0.373	0.329	0.292	0.260	0.198	0.153	0.120	0.095	0.077
5	0.476	0.437	0.402	0.341	0.291	0.250	0.215	0.186	0.132	0.095	0.070	0.053	0.040
6	0.410	0.370	0.335	0.275	0.227	0.189	0.158	0.133	0.088	0.060	0.041	0.029	0.021
7	0.354	0.314	0.279	0.222	0.178	0.143	0.116	0.095	0.059	0.037	0.024	0.016	0.011
8	0.305	0.266	0.233	0.179	0.139	0.108	0.085	0.068	0.039	0.023	0.014	0.009	0.006
9	0.263	0.226	0.194	0.144	0.108	0.082	0.063	0.048	0.026	0.015	0.008	0.005	0.003
10	0.227	0.191	0.162	0.116	0.085	0.062	0.046	0.035	0.017	0.009	0.005	0.003	0.002
11	0.195	0.162	0.135	0.094	0.066	0.047	0.034	0.025	0.012	0.006	0.003	0.002	0.001
12	0.168	0.137	0.112	0.076	0.052	0.036	0.025	0.018	0.008	0.004	0.002	0.001	0.001
13	0.145	0.116	0.093	0.061	0.040	0.027	0.018	0.013	0.005	0.002	0.001	0.001	0.000
14	0.125	0.099	0.078	0.049	0.032	0.021	0.014	0.009	0.003	0.001	0.001	0.000	0.000
15	0.108	0.084	0.065	0.040	0.025	0.016	0.010	0.006	0.002	0.001	0.000	0.000	0.000
16	0.093	0.071	0.054	0.032	0.019	0.012	0.007	0.005	0.002	0.001	0.000	0.000	0.000
17	0.080	0.060	0.045	0.026	0.015	0.009	0.005	0.003	0.001	0.000	0.000		0.000
18	0.069	0.051	0.038	0.021	0.012	0.007	0.004	0.002	0.001	0.000	0.000		0.000
19	0.060	0.043	0.031	0.017	0.009	0.005	0.003	0.002	0.000	0.000			0.000
20	0.051	0.037	0.026	0.014	0.007	0.004	0.002	0.001	0.000	0.000			
25	0.024	0.016	0.010	0.005	0.002	0.001	0.000	0.000					
30	0.012	0.007	0.004	0.002	0.001	0.000	0.000						

Answers to Study Tasks

1 The users of financial statements

1 Competitors, employees, suppliers, lenders, Inland Revenue, Customs and Excise

2 (a) Sales revenue from rooms, bar, restaurant and leisure complex; Expenses and costs for each department; profit achieved by each department

(b) Generally quarterly, with monthly updates.

(c)

Method	Advantages	Disadvantages
Staff meeting	• Everyone is given the information at the same time • Feedback is possible	• Possible disruption to operations by bringing all the staff together • Costly to the business as time is lost
Memo	• Information can be planned and clearly stated • Can be kept for reference	• Impersonal • Can be misunderstood
Newsletter	• Information is well presented • Regularly produced and circulated	• Not always read by everyone • Costly to produce • Limited coverage due to wider circulation

3 **Advantages of pie chart**
Easy to understand, summarises a good deal of information, demonstrates relationships of information, easy to produce with computer packages.

4 • Dealing with suppliers who are known to have a responsible attitude to the environment.
• Recycling own waste where possible.
• Minimising waste.
• Using recyclable products.
• Donations to groups linked with environmental concerns.

5   (a)   **Information required.**
  - Length of time the company has been in business.
  - Names of directors.
  - Bank account details.
  - Names of major customers.
  - Copy of annual accounts search at Companies House.
  (b)   **References**
  - Bank.
  - Other trade suppliers.
  - Credit reference agency.
6   **Information which would be useful**
  - Expenditure figures for domestic and international tourists.
  - Performance of competitors.
  - Level of investment in the hotel and leisure industries/trends.
  Sources of information
  - Tourism reports, e.g. BTA.
  - Annual Company Reports/On-line databases, e.g. Harvest.
  - Government/industry reports/trade journals.

2   Accounting concepts and conventions

1   **Realisation** – the sale is recorded when the invoice is raised, not when the cash is received.
2   **Materiality** – the amount is probably too small, i.e. it is under £100; or the expected life may be less than a year due to theft or breakage.
3   **Consistency** – when calculating depreciation the aim is to provide for the cost of using the asset over its working life and not its fall in market value.
4   **Entity** – in accounts the business and owners are treated as separate. The business therefore owes the money to the owners.
5   **Money measurement** – the accounts only show items of monetary value. The value of the chef to the business is subjective.
6   **Accruals** – expenses are treated as costs when incurred, not when they are eventually paid.

3   Establishing a financial record keeping system

1   (a)   Purchases Day Book.

(b) Petty Cash Book.
(c) Cash Book.
(d) Cash Book.
(e) Purchases Returns Book.
(f) Sales Day Book.
(g) Sales Returns Book.

2 Dr   **CASH BOOK**   Cr

Date	Cash £	Bank £	Date	Cash £	Bank £
March			**March**		
1 Opening balance	150		2 Postage	12	
3 Cash sales	30		4 Rent	18	
7 Cash sales	60		5 Wages	25	
8 Bank		80	6 Petrol	10	
			8 Paid cash into bank	80	
			9 Balance	95	80
	240	80		240	80
10 Balance	95	80			

3   **PETTY CASH BOOK**

Receipts	Folio	Date	Details	Vouch. No.	Total	Travel	Stationery	Flowers
£		**May**		–	£	£	£	£
100		1	Cash		1.60	1.60		
		2	Taxi fare		2.30		2.30	
		3	Envelopes		5.40	5.40		
		4	Taxi Fare		1.90		1.90	
		5	Pencils		9.80			9.80
		6	Flowers		2.40		2.40	
		7	Paper		3.80	3.80		
		8	Taxi fare					
					27.20	10.80	6.60	9.80
27.20		9	Cash					
		9	Balance	c/d	100.00			
127.20					127.20			
100		10	Balance b/d					

4 (a) Purchases Day Book

Date Sep	Supplier	Invoice No.	Folio	£
1	Jones and Sons			48
3	Peter Bright			274
7	David Morris			75
11	Hillars			54
16	Specialities			32
	Transferred to Purchases Account			483

(b) Sales Day Book

Date Sep	Supplier	Invoice No.	Folio	£
1	D&A Brothers			274
5	Mr and Mrs Sandhurst			882
8	Business Club			540
12	Excel Computers			69
15	Mr H. Kelly			485
	Transferred to Sales Account			2250

5 (a) Sales Returns Book

Date Sep	Customer	Credit Note No.	Folio	£
7	D&A Brothers			25
15	Business Club			75
	Transferred to Returns Inwards Account			100

(b) Purchases Returns Book

Date Sep	Supplier	Debit Note No.	Folio	£
7	Peter Bright			50
19	Specialities			10
	Transferred to Returns Outwards Account			60

6 (a) A *trade discount* is not shown in the accounts. It is money which is deducted from the cost of purchases because the buyer is a member of a particular trade and places large orders.

A *cash discount* is money which is deducted from a bill for prompt payment.

   (b) The Petty Cash Book is used for recording small incidental items of expenditure.

   (c) It is useful for management to know the precise amount of goods being sent back to suppliers and being received back from customers. The information is readily available for analysis and interpretation.

4 Preparing the Ledger Accounts

1 (a) Debit Bank, Credit Cash.
   (b) Debit Bank, Credit R. Green.
   (c) Debit Purchases, Credit Cash.
   (d) Debit Drawings, Credit Cash.
   (e) Debit Petrol, Credit Cash
   (f) Debit Rates, Credit Bank.

2 (a) Credit.
   (b) Debit.
   (c) Credit.
   (d) Debit.
   (e) Debit.
   (f) Credit.
   (g) Debit.
   (h) Debit
   (i) Debit.
   (j) Credit.

3 **Day**
    1 Debit Cash, Credit Bank.
    2 Debit Motor Repairs, Credit Cash.
    3 Debit Cash, Credit Sales, .
      Debit Bank, Credit Cash.
    4 Debit Wages, Credit Cash.
      Debit Newspapers, Credit Cash.
    5 Debit Cash, Credit Bank.
      Debit Purchases, Credit Cash.

4 **Day**
    1 Debit Purchases, Credit SeaWorld.
    2 Debit Tennis Club, Credit Sales.
    3 Debit Fixtures and Fittings; Credit Archers.
    4 Debit SeaWorld, Credit Bank.
    5 Debit Bank, Credit MiniComputer company.

5 (a) Credit.
   (b) Debit.
   (c) Debit.

(d) Debit.
(e) Debit.
(f) Credit.
(g) Credit.
(h) Debit.
(i) Debit.
(j) Debit.
(k) Debit.
(l) Debit.
(m) Debit.
(n) Debit.
(o) Debit.
(p) Debit.

6 **Trial Balance**

	Dr £	Cr £
Wages	1,500	
Heat and light	2,000	
Carriage inwards	400	
Cleaning	1,200	
Rates	900	
Discount received		400
Creditors		3,000
Motor expenses	1,000	
Capital		3,600
	7,000	7,000

5 Preparing a Trading and Profit and Loss Account

1 (a) Trading Account.
   (b) Profit and Loss Account.
   (c) Trading Account.
   (d) Profit and Loss Account.
   (e) Profit and Loss Account.
   (f) Profit and Loss Account.
   (g) Profit and Loss Account.
   (h) Trading Account.

    (i) Trading Account.
    (j) Profit and Loss Account.
    (k) Profit and Loss Account.
    (l) Trading Account.
    (m) Profit and Loss Account.
    (n) Trading Account.
    (o) Profit and Loss Account.
    (p) Profit and Loss Account.
    (q) Profit and Loss Account

2 Report examining why a profitable business may still be short of cash:
- Credit sales will mean no cash until debtor pays.
- An increase in activity must be financed out of current cash resources.
- The firm will increase investment in stock and debtors, thereby increasing cash.
- Cash may be needed to purchase extra fixed assets to cope with the expansion.

3 **Rowing machine**
    (a) Depreciation using the straight line method:

$$\frac{\text{Cost of asset} - \text{Residual value}}{\text{Expected useful life of asset}} = \frac{£2500 - 500}{4}$$

$$= £500 \text{ per annum}$$

    (b) Depreciation using the reducing balance method:
         Percentage depreciation to be charged:

$$1 - \sqrt[n]{\frac{s}{a}} \times 100$$

n = Life of asset
s = Residual value   £500 = the residual value of the rowing machine
a = Total installed cost   £2500 = the cost of the rowing machine

$$= 1 - \sqrt[4]{\frac{500}{2500}} \times 100$$

$$= 1 - \sqrt[4]{0.2} \times 100$$

$$= 1 - 0.669 \times 100$$
$$= 0.33125 \times 100 = 33.125\%$$

$$2500 - 828 \;=\; 1672$$
$$1672 - 554 \;=\; 1188$$
$$1118 - 370 \;=\; 748$$
$$748 - 248 \;=\; 500$$

4 When preparing accounts the sale is recorded when the invoice is raised – a provision is made for bad and doubtful debts. Similarly an expense is recorded when it is incurred, and not when it is paid.

5 The Valley View Bar: Trading Account
Net sales: £46,440
Cost of goods sold: £12,320
Gross profit: £34,120

6 The Victoria Restaurant: Trading Profit and Loss Account
Gross profit: £41,100
Total expenses: £40,700
Net profit: £400

6 Preparing a Balance Sheet

1 (a) Capital £45,000.
  (b) Fixed assets £10,000.
  (c) Current assets £45,000.
  (d) Current liabilities £15,000.
  (e) Capital £26,000.

2 (a) Revenue.
  (b) Capital.
  (c) Revenue.
  (d) Capital.
  (e) Capital.
  (f) Revenue.
  (g) Revenue.

3 **Net assets**: Total Assets less Liabilities (short and long term).
Accruals: Money owing.
Capital employed: Total amount of long-term money financing the business.
Working capital: The differrence between the current assets and current liabilities.
Shareholders' funds: Amount of money financing the business which belongs to the shareholders (share capital plus reserves).
Prepayments: Money paid in advance.

4 **Historical cost**: the purpose of preparing final accounts is not to determine the market value of a business.

5

Assets	£	Liabilities	£
Stock	500	Creditors	150
Cash	1250	Subscriptions	
Subscriptions		in advance	10
in arrears	30	Capital	**2030**
Building society	350		
Stationery	20		
Debtors	40		
	2190		2190

NB For a charity, a Balance Sheet is usually referred to as a 'Statement of Affairs' and the capital as the 'Accumulated Fund'. Subscriptions in advance are a liability because until the New Year they may have to be repaid.

6 (a) Net Assets £80,000.
   (b) Net Assets £140,000.
   (c) Current Assets £46,000; Net Assets £50,000.
   (d) Capital £160,000; Net Assets £160,000.
   (e) Current Liabilities £80,000; Net Assets £146,000.
   (f) Fixed Assets £80,000; Net Assets £90,000.

7 Preparing Bank Reconciliation Statements

1 Sarah and Kate must prepare a Bank Reconciliation Statement for two reasons. Firstly, because of timing differences and secondly, because of entries made on the bank statements which have not yet been recorded in the Cash Book – such as bank charges.

2 Interest charges.
Bank service charges.
Lodgements made by bank giro credit.
Payments made by direct debit.

3 Cheques received but not yet credited by the bank; cheque payments not yet presented.

4 Bank Reconciliation Statement

	£
Balance as per cash Book Cr	2,790.60
Add Uncollected cheque	78.50
	2,869.10
Less Transfer	131.60
	2,737.50

5

Cash Book

	£		£
Balance	1,849.20	Bank Charges	18.80
Debtor	200.00	Debtor	510.00
		Interest	800.00
		Balance	720.40
	2,049.20		2,049.20

Balance as per Cash Book		720.40
Add Unpresented cheques	1,310.96	
	318.80	
		1,629.76
		2,350.16
Less Uncollected cheque		1,894.00
Balance as per Bank Statement		456.16

6

Cash Book

	£		£
Balance	469	Bank charges	3.40
		Standing order	100.00
	469	Cheque	92.20
		Balance	273.40
			469.00

Balance Reconciliation Statement

Balance as per Cash Book		273.40
Add Unpresented cheques	163.20	
	100.00	
		263.20
		536.60
Less Uncollected cheque		157.00
Balance as per Bank Statement		379.60

8 Accounting for wages

1 Internal record card (P.11).
   If new staff do not have a P.45 then a P.15 must be completed.

2 **Catherine Jenkins**: a personal allowance; if her husband does not work
   she can claim the married couple's allowance.
   Hugh Roberts: a personal allowance, MIRAS relief on first £30,000 of
   mortgage, plus tax relief on pension payments.
   Elaine Bates: a personal allowance, and she may be entitled to the
   married couple's allowance; also entitled to tax relief on her mother's
   medical insurance.

3 Use current tax tables to answer this question.

4 Use information in answer to Question **3** above.

5 **Suggested layout of Wages Accounts**

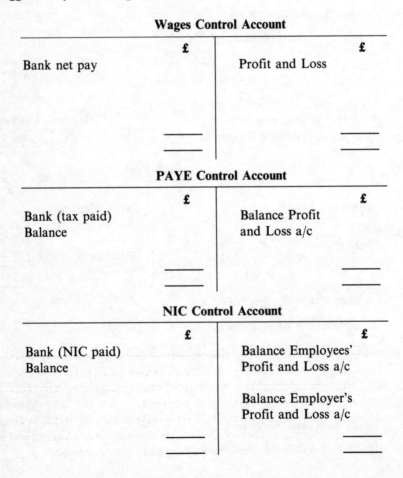

Wages Control Account

	£		£
Bank net pay		Profit and Loss	
	——		——
	——		——

PAYE Control Account

	£		£
Bank (tax paid)		Balance Profit	
Balance		and Loss a/c	
	——		——
	——		——

NIC Control Account

	£		£
Bank (NIC paid)		Balance Employees'	
Balance		Profit and Loss a/c	
		Balance Employer's	
		Profit and Loss a/c	
	——		——
	——		——

6 Leaving documents for Daphne: this depends on the time of year she leaves – if she departs during the tax year, a P.45 must be completed; if she leaves at the end of the tax year a P.60 must be completed (this is a three-part document – the employee receives one part and the second part goes to the tax authorities and is called a P.14)

9 Recording value added tax

1

		£	
Single beds:		106.38	
		18.62	(17½% VAT)
		125.00	

		£	
Double beds:		204.25	
		35.74	(17½% VAT)
		239.99	

		£	
Bunk beds:		127.66	
		22.34	(17½% VAT)
		150.00	

2

		£	
Lambswool:		35.00	
		6.13	
		41.13	(inc. 17½% VAT)

		£	
Aran:		25.00	
		4.38	
		29.38	(inc. 17½% VAT)

		£	
Lambswool and Cashmere		65.00	
		11.38	
		76.38	(inc. 17½% VAT)

3 VAT is a tax paid by the final customers. Businesses if registered for VAT must settle the difference between tax collected from customers and tax paid to suppliers. This means that sometimes a registered firm will owe tax and sometimes it will receive a rebate. Roger's tax position will depend on whether or not his business is registered and on the tax he has collected. If he is a registered business he will be entitled either to a refund or to offset the amount paid against the sum owed.

4 (a) £1,600
   (b) Sales Ledger, Bought Ledger and the Cash Book

5

	£
Debit Purchases	8,000
Debit VAT	1,200
Credit Bought Ledger Creditors	9,200
	£
Debit Sales Ledger Debtors	16,100
Credit Sales	14,000
Credit VAT	2,100

6 (a)

Debtors' Control Account

Yr 1	£	Yr 2	£
1 April balance B/F	12,000	31 March Bank	27,000
Yr 2			
31 March Sales	37,000		
		Discount allowed	1,300
		Balance C/F	20,700
	£49,000		£49,000

(b)

Creditors' Control Account

Yr 2	£	Yr 1	£
31 March Bank	14,300	1 April	
		Balance B/F	3,750
		Yr 2	
Discount	370		
Balance C/F	7,080	31 March	
		Purchases	18,000
	£21,750		£21,750

(c)

VAT Control Account

Yr 1	£	Yr 2	£
30 June Bank	1,400	1 April	
		Balance B/F	1,400
		Yr 2	
31 March VAT		31 March VAT	
on inputs	2,681	on output	5,511
Balance C/F	2,830		
	£6,911		£6,911

10 Preparing company accounts

1 Profit and Loss Account
   Income
   The hotel must provide details about its: turnover (sales), income from investments, rental income received (rents) and profit or loss on the sale of fixed assets.
   Expenses against profit
   Staff costs, directors' emoluments (income), employees' emoluments, interest payments, hire of plant, auditing fees, depreciation and reductions in the value of investments (write downs).
   Appropriation of profit (How profit is used)
   Taxation (Corporation Tax), reduction in goodwill, transfer to reserves and dividends paid.
   Notes to the Accounts
   Extraordinary items and abnormal items and changes in accounting procedures.

2 **The Directors' Report**
   Review of the business, results and dividends, share capital, market value of land and buildings, political and charitable contributions, fixed assets, employment of disabled persons, directors, events since the year end, future developments, research and development, employee information, health and safety.

3 **Croeso Hotel**
   Trading Profit and Loss Account for Year 2

	£	£
Sales		210,000
Opening stock	35,000	
Add: Purchases	80,000	
	115,000	
Less: Closing stock	15,000	
Cost of goods sold		100,000
Gross profit		110,000
Discount received		500
Interest received		200
		110,700
Wages	70,000	
Insurance	3,000	
Heating and lighting	6,000	
Postage and telephone	1,000	

	£	£
Gardening	2,000	
Audit fee	1,700	
Rates	6,000	
Motor expenses	2,000	
Advertising	1,500	
Printing and stationery	3,500	
Repairs and renewals	5,000	101,700
Net Profit		9,000

3   Croeso Hotel
Balance Sheet as at end of Year 2

	£	£	£
Fixed Assets			
Hotel			140,000
Furniture, fixtures and fittings			20,000
			160,000
Current Assets			
Stock	15,000		
Debtors	44,000		
	59,000		
Less Current Liabilities			
Creditors	20,000		
Working capital			39,000
			199,000
Less Long Term Liabilities			
Mortgage		40,000	
Bank loan		10,000	
			50,000
Net assets			149,000
Financed by:			
140,000 Ordinary £1 shares			140,000
Profit and Loss Account			9,000
			149,000

4 The Croeso Hotel
Profit and Loss Account for Year 2
(for presentation in a published corporate report)

	£	£
Turnover		210,000
Trading profit	9,000	
Interest received	2,000	
Profit on ordinary		
activities before taxation	9,200	

NB The Balance Sheet would appear in the same format as presented in the answer to Question **3** above.

5 The proceeds of the sale of the shares would be split to show the money received from the sale. This would be the nominal value per share multiplied by the number sold. The proceeds above the nominal value would be shown as a premium and would be entered in the Balance Sheet as a reserve under the heading 'Share Premium'.

A capital reserve cannot be used to pay dividends whereas a revenue reserve can be used to pay them. Capital reserves are sometimes referred to as statutory reserves, because the Companies Acts state how they may be used.

6 The share value will be influenced by the assets of the business and their ability to generate earnings.

11 Preparing cash flow statements

1 Report on cash flow position
   (a) Increase in current assets – stock and debtors.
   (b) Large investment in fixed assets.
   (c) Repayment of loan.
   (d) Decrease in creditors.

2 In the long term by increasing its level of sales.
   Reducing investment in current assets stocks and debtors.
   Increase in creditors.

3 **Creditors** – Shows that the business is generating cash which can be used to meet its current liabilities.
   Investors – Increase in cash flow means that the firm could pay bigger dividends. Cash left in the business will increase

shareholder wealth because it should earn higher returns from the additional investment.

Managers – An increase in cash shows that the business is being well managed. A business must be able to generate cash from its trading.

Employees – Job security; possibility of a higher pay rise; satisfaction of working for a successful company.

4 (a) Application.   (f) Application.
   (b) Application.   (g) Source.
   (c) Source.   (h) Source.
   (d) Application.   (i) Source.
   (e) Source.   (j) Source.

5 **Cash flow statement for the year ended 31 December Year 2**

	£	£
Cash flow from operating activities		14,000
Investing activities		
Payments to acquire tangible fixed assets		(54,000)
		40,000
Financing		
Issue of Ord. shares	20,000	
Long-term loans	30,000	
Increase in cash		50,000
		10,000
Reconciliation of operating profit to net cash flow investment from operating activities		
Operating profit		56,000
Increase in stock		(24,000)
Increase in debtors		(20,000)
Increase in creditors		2,000
Net cash flow from operating activities		14,000

	Year 2	Year 1	Change in Cr.
	£	£	£
Increase in cash and cash equivalents			
Cash or bank and in hand	26,000	16,000	10,000

6 Memo explaining cash flow figures

The bakery has increased its cash by £10,000. It has raised £50,000 from outside sources and invested £54,000 in new fixed assets.

The business has increased its stock and debtors and has financed this partly by increasing its creditors.

12 Cost behaviour and control

1	(a)	Direct.		(e)	Direct.
	(b)	Indirect.		(f)	Direct.
	(c)	Direct.		(g)	Indirect.
	(d)	Indirect.		(h)	Indirect.

2 Variable cost per meal: £6.25; £6.25; £6.25; £6.25; £6.25; £6.25.

3

No. of visitors	Fixed Cost per Guest £
0	2,000
10	200
50	40
100	20
150	13.33
200	10
250	8
500	4
750	2.66
1,000	2.00

4

	50%	60%	70%	80%	90%	100%
Guests	150	180	210	240	270	300
	£	£	£	£	£	£
Food costs	1,350	1,620	1,890	2,160	2,430	2,700
Direct labour	450	540	630	720	810	900
Drink	300	360	420	480	540	600
Fixed costs	900	900	900	900	900	900
Total costs	3,000	3,420	3,840	4,260	4,680	5,100
Sales	2,250	2,700	3,150	3,600	4,050	4,500
Profit (loss)	(750)	(720)	(690)	(660)	(630)	(600)

5

	May	Jun	Jul	Aug
Bar food costs	£3,675	£4,200	£5,040	£6,510
Customers	1750	2000	2400	3,100
Cost per meal	£2.10	£2.10	£2.10	£2.10
Alcohol	£2,485	£2,840	£3,408	£4,402
Customers	1750	2000	2400	3100
Cost per drink	£1.42	£1.42	£1.42	£1.42

Calculation of overheads		Cost £	Activity
	Highest	2,960	3,100
	Lowest	2,150	1,750
		810	1,350

$$\frac{\text{Cost}}{\text{Activity}} \quad \frac{£810}{1,350} = \text{60p per unit variable cost of overhead}$$

	May	Jun	Jul	Aug
Total overheads	£2,150	2,300	2,540	2,960
Unit variable cost 60p × output	£1,050	1,200	1,440	1,860
Fixed costs	£1,100	1,100	1,100	1,100

6

	Jan	Feb	Mar	Apr	May	Jun
Food	£5,920	£5,550	£10,360	£13,320	£16,280	£19,980
Covers	800	750	1400	1800	2200	2700
Cost per meal	£7.40	£7.40	£7.40	£7.40	£7.40	£7.40
Alcohol	£2,480	£2,325	£4,340	£5,580	£6,820	£8,370
Covers	800	750	1400	1800	2200	2700
Cost per unit	£3.10	£3.10	£3.10	£3.10	£3.10	£3.10
Labour	£2,000	£1,875	£3,500	£4,500	£5,500	£6,750
Covers	800	750	1400	1800	2200	2700
Cost put unit	£2.50	£2.50	£2.50	£2.50	£2.50	£2.50

Calculation of overheads

	Cost £	Activity
Highest	6,780	2,700
Lowest	4,050	750
	2,730	1,950

$$\frac{\text{Cost}}{\text{Activity}} \quad \frac{£2,730}{1,950} = £1.40 \text{ per unit variable cost of overhead}$$

	£	£	£	£	£	£
Total overheads	4,120	4,050	4,960	5,520	6,080	6,780
Unit variable cost £1.40 × output	1,120	1,050	1,960	2,520	3,080	3,780
Fixed costs	3000	3000	3000	3000	3,000	3,000

	Jan £	Feb £	Mar £	Apr £	May £	Jun £
Sales	14,400	13,500	25,200	32,400	39,600	48,600
Less Variable costs	10,400	9,750	18,200	23,400	28,600	35,100
Contribution	4,000	3,750	7,000	9,000	11,000	13,500
Less fixed costs	3,000	3,000	3,000	3,000	3,000	3,000
Profit	1,000	750	4,000	6,000	8,000	10,500

13 Cost analysis and decision making

1 Output method

$$\frac{\text{Total overhead for cost centre}}{\text{Number of cost units produced}} \quad \frac{£70,000}{40,000} = £1.75$$

Labour hours

$$\frac{\text{Total overhead for cost centre}}{\text{Number of labour hours}} \quad \frac{£70,000}{3,500} = £20$$

Machine Hours

$$\frac{\text{Total overhead for cost centre}}{\text{Number of machine hours}} \quad \frac{£70,000}{1,200} = £58.33$$

2 (a) Cost of ice making machine. Other costs are not related to the decision and so they are irrelevant.
   (b) The costs foregone. Money invested in the ice-making machine cannot be invested elsewhere.
   (c) Past costs which are not relevant to the present decision.

3

		Beef		Duck		Chicken
		£	£	£	£	£
Selling price		14		12		10
Less variable costs						
Food costs	6		5		4	
Direct labour	3		2		2	
Variable overheads	2		1		1	
Total variable cost		11		8		7
Contribution		3		4		3

4 (a)

		Gateau		Trifle
	£	£	£	£
Selling price		5.00		4.50
Less variable costs				
Food costs	2.00		1.50	
Labour	1.50		1.00	
		3.50		2.50
Contribution		1.50		2.00

(b)

	£	£
Contribution	1.50	2.00
Time	2 hr	1 hr
Contribution per hour	0.75	2.00

It would be best to make the trifle.

5

	£
Selling price	8.00
Less variable costs	4.50
Contribution	3.50

$$\frac{\text{Fixed Costs}}{\text{Contribution}} \quad \frac{15,000}{3.50} = 4286 \text{ per year}$$

$$\frac{\text{Fixed costs}}{\text{Weeks}} \quad \frac{£1,500}{52} = £288 \text{ per week}$$

$$\frac{\text{Fixed costs}}{\text{Contribution}} \quad \frac{288}{3.50} = 82 \text{ customers per week}$$

6 (a)

		£
Selling Price		9.00
Less variable costs		
Food	2.50	
Labour	1.25	
Drinks	2.00	5.75
Contribution		3.25

(b) Break even: $\dfrac{\text{Fixed costs}}{\text{Contribution}} \dfrac{£800}{3.25} = 246 \text{ guests}$

(c)

	£	£
Sales 200 @ £9		1,800
Less variable costs:		
Food	500	
Labour	250	
Drinks	400	
Total variable costs		1,150
Contribution		650
Less fixed costs		800
Loss		(150)

14 Managing budgets

1

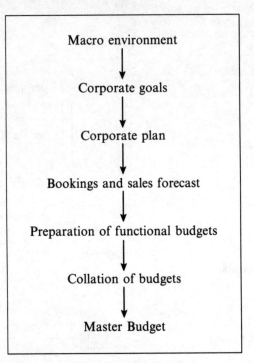

Macro environment

↓

Corporate goals

↓

Corporate plan

↓

Bookings and sales forecast

↓

Preparation of functional budgets

↓

Collation of budgets

↓

Master Budget

2 **Benefits of a budgetary control system:**
- Staff will have control over their budget heads
- Helps to keep control of the business and ensure it does not have cash flow problems
- Allows action to be taken as appropriate
- Ensures events conform to plan
- Optimises resources.

3 **Type of limiting factors**
  (a) Internal limiting factor for the restaurant
      External limiting factor for the kitchen
  (b) **Overcoming limiting factors**
      - Expand the restaurant
      - Seek to increase demand for functions by increasing marketing effort or decreasing price.

4   Cash Budget

	Jan £	Feb £	Mar £	Apr £	May £	Jun £
Receipts:						
Bar: Cash sales	12,000	14,000	16,500	18,000	16,750	19,000
Leisure Complex: Cash sales	500	1,200	1,400	2,000	2,300	2,400
Restaurant: Cash sales	21,000	25,200	28,200	31,200	28,800	33,000
Restaurant: Credit sales	–	14,000	16,800	18,800	20,800	19,200
Rooms: Cash sales	24,000	28,200	33,000	39,000	46,800	51,000
Rooms: Credit sales	–	16,000	18,800	22,000	26,000	31,200
Total Income	**57,500**	**98,600**	**114,700**	**131,000**	**141,450**	**155,800**
Payments:						
Food costs	17,500	21,000	23,500	26,000	24,000	27,500
Beverage costs	6,000	7,000	8,250	9,000	8,375	9,500
Lease	700	700	700	700	700	700
Fixed costs	3,125	3,125	3,125	3,125	3,125	3,125
	–	9,375	9,375	9,375	9,375	9,375
Tax				34,000		
Total Expenditure	**27,325**	**41,200**	**44,950**	**82,200**	**45,575**	**50,200**
Opening balance	45,000	75,175	132,575	202,325	251,125	347,000
Total income	57,500	98,600	114,700	131,000	141,450	155,800
Less: Total expenditure	27,325	41,200	44,950	82,200	45,575	50,200
Closing Balance	**75,175**	**132,575**	**202,325**	**251,125**	**347,000**	**452,600**

5   Budget Profit and Loss Account

	£	£
Sales: Restaurant	279,000	
Contribution		139,500
Sales: Bar	96,250	
Contribution		48,125
	375,250	187,625
Less: Leasing payment	4,200	
Fixed costs	30,000	
		34,200
Profit		153,425

6

Room Type	Rate per person	Rate per room	No. rooms	Revenue at 100% occupancy
	£	£		£
Single	52.50	52.50	16	840
Standard double	40.00	80.00	18	1440
Luxury double	45.00	90.00	4	360
Suite	62.50	125.00	2	250
Total revenue at 100% occupancy for one night				**£2,890**

Level of occupancy	Budgeted sales revenue per night
%	£
100	2,890
90	2,601
80	2,312
70	2,023
60	1,734
50	1,445

15   Establishing a standard costing and variance analysis system

1   Benefits of a standard costing system
   - Unit costs should be reduced because of improvements made in their control.
   - Stock control procedures should be simplified because food and beverages can be valued at their standard cost. This method is easier than valuing stock on a Last in First Out (LIFO) or First in First Out (FIFO) basis, for example.
   - Price setting should be improved because the hotel has accurate information about its costs.
   - The system highlights variances from standards and Sarah and Kate are able to focus on that analysis. There is, therefore, no need to spend time in analysing costs which are performing to standard – the system allows management by exception.
   - The hotel can benefit from establishing new working practices by reconsidering these before the standards are set.

How the standards should be set
Before a standard costing system can be established it is necessary to gather information on food and beverage prices, wage rates and overhead expenses. With this data a standard is set for each cost based on either a normal or ideal standard.

2 • Direct material usage variance: Flour
   Formula: (Standard quantity specified for actual production – Actual quantity used) × Standard price
   (1,500kg – 1,800kg) × 45p per kg
   = (300kg) × 45p
   = (£135 adverse)

   • **Direct material usage variance: Cream**
   (500 pints – 425 pints) × 64p per pint
   = 75 pints × 64p
   = £48 favourable

3 • Direct labour variance: cleaning conference room
   Formula:
   (Standard direct labour hours produced × standard rate per hour) –
   (Actual direct labour hours worked × Actual rate per hour)
   4 hours × £3.50 per hour   = £14.00 Standard cost
   3 hours × £3.50 per hour   = £10.50 Actual cost

   = £ 3.50 favourable

   • **Direct labour variance: cleaning beer cellar**
   1 hour × £6 per hour   = £6.00 Standard cost
   1½ hours × £4 per hour   = £6.00 Actual cost

   = £ –

4 • Direct material price variance: orange juice
   Formula: Actual quantity purchased × (Standard price – Actual price)

   2,400 bottles × (60p – 66p)
   2,400 × (0.06p)
   = (£144 adverse)

   • Direct material price variance: milk
   425 pints × (64p – 62p)
   425 × 0.02
   = £8.50 favourable

5 The Croeso Hotel
Profit and Loss Account (for the first quarter)

	Budgeted £	Actual £
Sales	337,500	303,750
Less:		
Materials	180,000	102,000
Labour	90,000	61,500
Overheads	45,000	24,000
Variable cost	315,000	187,500
Budgeted profit	22,500	116,250
		22,500
Sales variance adverse	(33,750)	
Materials variance favourable	78,000	
Labour variance favourable	28,500	
Overheads variance favourable	21,000	
		(93,750)
Actual profit		93,750

6 The costs involved in running the front office will include materials such as stationery, pens and brochures; labour and overheads such as insurance. If Catherine Jenkins calculates the standard and actual costs and concludes that the variances are all favourable it means that the costs of running the department were less than had been budgeted.

   Although this result may appear good to inexperienced management it is important that **any** variance from standard be investigated, not just those which are adverse. This is because the underlying reasons for a favourable variance may be detrimental for the business in the long term.

16 Interpreting financial accounts

1 Upper quartile, median and lower quartile are statistical measures of dispersion with the median corresponding to the average. The upper quartile is above the median and the lower quartile below it.

- **Current ratio**   – broad measure of liquidity.
- **Acid test**   – Narrow measure of liquidity.

- **Stock turnover** shows the number of times during a financial year that the stock is sold. The higher the stock turnover generally, the more profitable the business and the less liquid it needs to be.

- **Sales to debtors**   –   shows how long it takes the firm to collect its debts.

- **Return on capital**   –   the higher the return, the more effectively the management use the capital which is financing the business.

- **Earnings per share** –   an accounting measure of return, and shows what each share invested in the business can earn.

- **Dividend yield**   –   shows the return which a shareholder receives from owning a share in the business.

- **Gearing**   –   measures the ratio of debt to share capital. The higher the level of gearing the higher the level of financial risk.

2 (a) The amount of cash and near cash such as debtors which a business has which can be used to pay its current liabilities.

  (b) Current ratio – broad measure or narrow measure. Acid test ratio.

  (c) Reduce stock levels, minimum and maximum stock levels. Set optimum re-order levels. Minimise investment in debtors. Take advantage of credit terms. Invest surplus cash in interest earning deposits.

3 Increase in share capital financing the company and a reduction in loan capital, therefore reduction in financial risk to investors. Increase in sales. Decrease in gross profits but increase on capital employed. Marginal decrease in liquidity despite reduction in stock and debtors.

4 The figures show an expanding and profitable business as measured by the accounting measures of profit. This growth is being financed by higher levels of debt. This increase in gearing exposes the shareholders to a greater degree of financial risk.

5 • **Financial performance**: How effective a firm is at using its assets to generate a financial return. This is normally measured by the ratio return on capital employed.

- **Measuring financial performance**: It enables management to compare their results with companies of similar size operating in the same markets.
- **Financial Ratios used to Measure Business Effectiveness**: Current ratio, acid test, Stock turnover, Debtors collection, Return on capital employed.

- **Reliance on ratios**: Based on past information. They should be used to enable management to focus on the financial strengths and weaknesses of the business.

6 (1) "Gearing" is the term used to describe the ratio of equity to debt capital. RoundTours is an all-equity company. LuxTravel is a geared company. The ratio is 1:1, i.e. £1 of share capital for each £ of debt capital.

  (2) Increasing the level of borrowing increases the financial risk to shareholders when they purchase shares in LuxTravel. The shares in RoundTours are a less risky investment because it has no debt capital. From the information, given both companies would appear an attractive investment but no equity investment can be regarded as a risk-free investment.

17 Managing working capital

1 "Working capital" is the difference between the current assets and current liabilities of a business. It is the term used to describe a firm's short-term use of funds. It is needed to purchase food, beverages and other items for the hotel and to pay expenses. If the working capital is not sufficient the hotel will not be able to continue trading.

2 **Maximum stock level of white wine**
Re-order level – (minimum usage × minimum lead time) + re-order quantity

Re-order level $\qquad$ = maximum usage × maximum lead time
$\qquad\qquad\qquad\qquad$ = 300 litres × 4 weeks = 1,200 litres

1,200 – (100 × 3) + 1,000 = **1,900 litres**

Maximum stock level of red wine
Re-order level $\qquad\qquad$ = 300 litres × 3 weeks = 900 litres

900 – (100 × 2) + 1,250 $\quad$ = **1,950 litres**

Minimum stock level of white wine
Re-order level – (average usage × average lead time)

1,200 litres – (200 × 3.5 weeks) = **500 litres**

Minimum stock level of red wine
900 – (200 × 2.5) = **400 litres**

3   High-protein drink
Re-order level
Maximum usage × maximum lead time
= 150 packets × 4 weeks
= **600 packets**

Maximum stock level
Re-order level – (minimum usage × minimum lead time) + re-order quantity
= 600 – (50 × 2) + 500
= **1,000 packets**

Minimum stock level
Re-order level – (average usage × average lead time)
600 – (100 × 3)
= **300 packets**

Average stock level
Minimum stock level + ½ re-order quantity
300 + 250
= **550 packets**

4   (1)   Current interest cost to the firm

$$\frac{2}{98} \times \frac{365}{(30 - 14)\text{days}} = 47\%$$

(2)   Proposed interest cost to the firm

$$\frac{2}{98} \times \frac{365}{(60 - 30)\text{days}} = 25\%$$

5   Procedures that should be followed before giving customers credit:
- Credit references.
- Credit scoring.
- Monitoring debtor balances.
- Credit rating debtors.

6 Cash operating cycle diagram for Croeso Hotel

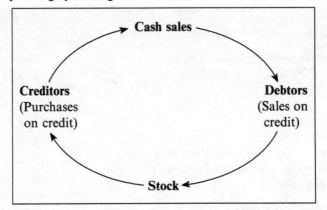

If the hotel buys too much on credit and does not receive cash from its debtors, it runs the risk of being unable to pay its expenses.

18 Appraising capital investment programmes

1 Factors to be considered before investing £1500 on the grounds:
The payback time; opportunity cost of the investment; return on investment.

2 ● Food mixer

Time (Years)	Cash inflows £	Total inflows £	Initial investment £
0	–	–	(450)
1	260	260	
2	410	670	

The payback time occurs between years 1 and 2.
£450 – £260 = £190 shortfall

$$\frac{£410}{12} = £34.20 \text{ (rounded up)}$$

$$\frac{£190}{£34.20} = 5.5 \text{ months}$$

The payback time is 1 year and 6 months (rounded up) for the food mixer

- Dishwasher

Time (years)	Cash inflows £	Total inflows £	Initial investment £
0	–	–	(1200)
1	450	450	
2	600	1050	
3	800	1850	

The payback time occurs between years 2 and 3.

£1200 – £1050 = £150 shortfall

$$\frac{£800}{12} = £66.70 \text{ (rounded up)}$$

$$\frac{£150}{£66.70} = 2.25 \text{ months (rounded up)}$$

The payback time is 2 years (rounded down) for the dishwasher

- Deep freeze

Time (years)	Cash inflows £	Total inflows £	Initial investment £
0	–	–	(1700)
1	300	300	
2	450	750	
3	500	1250	
4	700	1950	

The payback time occurs between years 3 and 4.

£1700 – £1250 = £450 shortfall

$$\frac{£700}{12} = £58.33$$

$$\frac{£450}{£58.33} = 7.7 \text{ months}$$

The payback time is 3 years and 8 months (rounded up)

3   Fax machine

Total cash flows for three years:	£3,700
Less initial investment:	£2,500
Profit	£1,200

Average profit = $\dfrac{£1,200}{3 \text{ yrs}}$ = £400

The accounting rate of return = $\dfrac{£400}{£2,500}$ × 100 = 16%

4

Time	Cash inflow	Discount factor	D/F	NPV
	£	%		£
1	3,000	10	0.909	2727
4	10,000	12	0.636	6360
6	5,000	8	0.630	3150
9	60,000	14	0.308	18480
3	20,000	20	0.579	11580
15	44,000	16	0.108	4752

Memo

The time value of money should always be considered before investing because:

Money has an opportunity cost which is the lost interest caused by the time delay in receiving the money. The discount factor should reflect the firm's cost of capital. Therefore only those projects which have an NPV of zero or higher can earn such a return.

5   Net cash flow

Year	Investment	Cash inflow	Savings	Taxation	Net cash flow
	£	£	£	£	£
0	(25,000)	–	–	–	(25,000)
1	(1,500)	9,000	1,200	(500)	8,200
2	(2,000)	14,000	2,000	(700)	13,300
3	(500)	16,000	1,000	(950)	15,550
4	–	20,000	1,000	(1,400)	19,600

Year	Net cash flow £	Discount factor 12%	Net present value £
0	(25,000)	–	(25,000)
1	8,200	0.893	7,323
2	13,300	0.797	10,600
3	15,550	0.712	11,072
4	19,600	0.636	12,466

Net Present Value: **16,461**

6

Year	Net cash flow £	Discount factor 16%	Net present value £
0	(25,000)	–	(£25,000)
1	8,200	0.862	7,068
2	13,300	0.743	9,882
3	15,550	0.641	9,968
4	19,600	0.552	10,819

Net Present Value: **12,737**

19 Raising finance

1 (a) Business plan.
  (b) Annual accounts.
  (c) Budgeted Profit and Loss Account.
  (d) Cash Budget.
  (e) The payback time and NPV of the investment.

2 Interest charges of using factor house: $\dfrac{30 \times £28,500 \times 12\%}{365}$

Interest cost £281.09

3 $\dfrac{30 \times £12,000 \times 12\%}{365}$

	£
Interest cost	118.35
Handling charge	30.00
30p × 100	
Total cost	148.35

4

Sources	Advantages	Disadvantages
Bank loan	Fixed term	Inflexible
Mortgage	Fixed term	Surrender control of assets
Bank overdraft	Relatively inexpensive	Payable on demand
Factoring debts	Improves cash flow	Expensive
Leasing assets	Use of assets more important than ownership	Can be costly

5 (a) **Cost of capital before loan**

Capital	Proportion %	Cost %	Cost × Proportion %
Equity	62.5	12	7.50
Debt	37.5	10	3.75
Weighted average cost of capital			11.25

(b) **Cost of capital after loan**

Capital	Proportion %	Cost %	Cost × Proportion %
Equity	50	12	6
Debt	30	10	3
Debt	20	14	2.8
Weighted average cost of capital			11.8%

6 (a) New level of gearing

$$\frac{\text{Debt} \quad £250,000}{\text{Equity} \quad £250,000} = 1.1$$

(b) The hotel must be able to generate sufficient profits to meet the additional interest cost. The cash flows will be effected by the interest payments. Net cash flows will only increase if profits rise to take account of the additional cash outflows brought about by the higher level of borrowing. If cash flows increase, the gain will benefit the shareholders as they can either be used to pay dividends or be used to reinvest in the business.

20 Managing foreign exchange

1 Sterling to be paid to guests

	£
German DM	326.53
US$	649.35
French Franc	79.91
Swiss Franc	375.00
Dutch Guilder	571.43

2 Sterling cost of foreign exchange for Kate

	£
German DM	836.82
Swiss Franc	500.00
French Franc	94.12

3 Three risks the hotel is exposed to
- Business risk.
- Financial risk.
- Foreign exchange risk.

4 Reasons why foreign exchange rates alter
- Effects of supply and demand.
- Economic variables – balance of payments, inflation.

Hedging strategies
- Buy currency in spot market and place in an interest bearing foreign currency account.
- Enter into a forward contract.
- Enter into an option contract.

5 (a) Sterling cost of software

Spot	1.7550
Premium	0.0007
	1.7543

$3,000 ÷ 1.7543 = **£1,710.08**

(b) The firm knows exactly what the costs will be once it has entered into the forward contract.

6 (a) Receipts from American tour company

Spot   1.7530
Premium   0.0011
          _____
          1.7519

$4000 ÷ 1.7519 = **£2,283.24**

(b) As sterling appreciates against the dollar the hotel receives less pounds on conversion. This is why a forward contract will be advantageous if this trend continues.

Index